# How To
# Care For
# Your Aging Parents...
# AND STILL
# HAVE A LIFE
# OF YOUR OWN!

by
J. Michael Dolan

Published By:
**MulHolland
Pacific** ⌂
Los Angeles, California

*How To Care For Your Aging Parents...*
**AND STILL HAVE A LIFE OF YOUR OWN!**

**By J. Michael Dolan**

Published By:
**Mulholland Pacific**
P.O. Box 93879
Los Angeles, CA 90093
(818) 558-1460

Manufactured in the United States Of America

**First printing**

**ISBN** 1-880867-13-3

**Library of Congress Catalog Number:** 92-60126

**Dedicated to the five JMD's:**
John Michael
Jean Margaret
Judi Marie
Joseph Michael
Juliann "Sam" Marie

# ENTWINED

It wasn't supposed to be this way.
You were always going to be
A combination of your best moments,
Teaching me, consoling me,
Sharing wisdom I was free to ignore
As I tried to grow into myself.
You were going to take your strength,
Your mind, your gentle humor with you.

It wasn't supposed to be this way.
When did you first look to me for answers,
Or for healing your fears
Of being alone, of forgetting, of falling?
How did I get control of your life?
(How did you get control of mine?)
I don't remember changing places.
Who are you to need me this badly?

It wasn't supposed to be this way.
I'm beginning to feel my life
Slipping through the cracks
Into errands and doctor visits
And the time I spend just out of guilt
With nothing constructive to offer,
Wishing I could heal your dying body
With some flowers or a game of catch.

It wasn't supposed to be this way.
Who am I to refuse the smallest,
Silliest request you can make,
To say no to the one who said yes so often?
I want you well, I want you young,
I want you dead, I want out of this,
I want my life back,
I want you to know I love you.

It wasn't supposed to be this way.
Some days I am good at this,
Calmly holding back eternity
With a squeeze of your hand;
Some days I am selfish and shame-ridden,
Unwilling to meet your eyes,
Fighting the impulse to run.
Both, I am learning, are me.

It wasn't supposed to be this way.
I am caring the best way I can,
The way you've told me you did,
And we are both where we need to be,
Sorting through the motions,
Wound inextricably in each other,
In the tiny details of the moment
That entwines your life with mine.

— Rob Simbeck

# Quick Reference
## Contents

# Part I: Personal

## 1. THE FACTS SPEAK FOR THEMSELVES ....27
**Main Focus**
You never thought this scenario would ever happen to you. Various stats and insights on the phenomena of parent care.
**Highlights**
• It is estimated that you could care for your parents for the next 10 to 25 years.
• The "baby boom" generation will reach 65 between the years 2010 and 2030.
• Recent studies have shown that most U.S. families are very good at caring for their elderly; only 5% of our senior citizen population lives in institutions or nursing homes.

## 2. ABOUT YOU ........................................................31
**Main Focus**
How to live "your life first" and still provide competent, efficient care for your parents.
**Highlights**
• Don't become so consumed by your parents' circumstances that you neglect your own.
• Give up trying to *prove* to them that you are a grown-up. Stop *acting* like the kid you used to be and start *interacting* with them like an adult.
• There is no reason to give in to the *unreasonable* demands of your parents, just as you would not do so with your children.

# *Quick Reference*
## Contents

**Main Focus**

How to, once and for all, let go of the guilt we carry around regarding our parents.

**Highlights**

• Guilt rips off your vitality and provides no room for positive action.

• Don't make yourself crazy by manifesting "guilt feelings" about imaginary scenarios in your head. You must remain stress-free if you intend to get through this and outlive them!

• Express your guilt-crazed thoughts to a best friend, close relative, or a therapist.

**Main Focus**

They never thought this would ever happen to them. A close look at the person your parent has become.

**Highlights**

• The "squirm"

• What your parents are afraid of

• What they've got to lose

• The manipulative games they play

**Main Focus**

Your parents are not interested in going for the ride if there is no chance to reach for the brass ring.

**Highlights**

• Ideas to pique your creative juices enough to sit down with your parents and come up with some reasons to keep them more involved in their own life, without having to invade yours.

• You *can* teach an old dog new tricks. Your parents *are* coachable and trainable.

# Quick Reference
## Contents

**Main Focus**

The strain and sadness of caring for difficult parents.

**Highlights**

• To achieve any kind of satisfactory working relationship with your stubborn parent, you need to be compassionately ruthless!

• Don't fall into the "I'm still your parent" trap. They may still be your parents, but they no longer have the right to boss you around, give you orders, or emotionally abuse you.

• Perhaps they are disappointed that their life didn't turn out the way they wanted. By abusing you, they are actually punishing themselves.

**Main Focus**

Taking charge of your parents' life without their knowledge and/or permission.

**Highlights**

• How and when to intervene

• All family members should be aware of the intervention

**Main Focus**

How to communicate with your parents in such a way that produces results.

**Highlights**

• Distinguishing random opinion from actual truth.

• Re-training ourselves to replace "complaining," which only provokes more upset, with "requesting," which actually invites resolve.

• Be committed to resolving the dispute, not to winning it.

# *Quick Reference*
## Contents

# Quick Reference
## Contents

# Quick Reference
## Contents

# Quick Reference
## Contents

# PREFACE

If you are currently caring for your aging parents, I want to acknowledge you. The burden of caring for your parents, while at the same time being responsible for your own personal life and family, can result in physical and emotional stress, family mayhem, and unceasing frustration. So, I admire your courage and I honor your dedication and commitment to the competent, loving care of your parents.

There are a few books that pay close attention to the needs of the elderly, but this book was written with you in mind. The purpose of this book is to introduce you to a new relationship with your aging parents, out of which you can learn to take optimum care of them and still maintain a personal life of your own. Since there are a variety of new circumstances in both your lives, it stands to reason there are just as many challenging options to help deal with them. The intent of this book is to point out those options.

## The format

This book was written in such a way that you do not have to read it from cover to cover to appreciate and get value from it. Simply scan the "Quick Reference Contents" for the topic you are currently confronting in your life. Most chapters are followed by a few recommendations that should prove to be helpful. My purpose is not to teach you something new, rather my goal is to simply remind you of what you already know.

For the sake of grammar, and since there are a variety of scenarios, (one parent deceased, two "sets" of parents, etc.), I use the terms "parents" or "parent" wherever it seems appropriate to do so. Also, to save the monotony of over using the term "him/her," I occasionally (and with much due respect to women) use "him" to express a generic gender, because this pronoun is commonly used as a recognizable idiom in the syntax of our culture.

This book is simple common sense. If you and your friends exchanged ideas on how to handle aging parents, you would most likely come up with many of the same suggestions. I have also discovered that people are eager to share their experiences and discuss their opinions about aging parents. Talking about it with others who are experiencing similar problems is terrific therapy.

Do not loan this book to anyone! Keep it as a reference, make notes in the margin, highlight certain sections and dog-ear the pages. You'll be surprised how often you refer to this book for a quick fix of information or support. On the other hand, you may know someone who is currently entangled in the parent/adult-child web, so I suggest you share with them the information on page 205.

**The information in this book is sourced from:**
• My own personal experience.
• Intimate conversations with my friends and family.
• Interviews with a variety of people currently facing this dilemma.
• Brochures and pamphlets from a multitude of government agencies, private organizations, and local senior citizen's organizations (see Appendix).
• The American Academic Encyclopedia, found on the computer network "Prodigy."
• *American Heritage Dictionary.*
• *Webster's New Revised Dictionary.*

**Disclaimer**
This book was written for average people with an average amount of family dysfunction. The opinions in this book are my own. They are not intended, in any way, to be therapeutic. Any recommendations that I have suggested are to be carried out at your own risk. If you have deep-seated problems with your parents, if they abused or abandoned you as a child, or you come from an alcoholic or dysfunctional family, you should seek professional help. This book is not a substitute for professional medical, psychological, or legal advice.

**Author's note:** There is a plethora of information regarding the care of the elderly which I obtained from private organizations, government agencies, and local community senior centers. I have taken extra measures to research the accuracy of that information and report it in such a way that is concise and readable. Given that there is so much information available, any similarity to a previously published work is purely coincidental.

# ACKNOWLEDGEMENTS

There is always a supporting cast in any production, and this book is no exception. My love and gratitude go out to the following very special people in my life:

Thanks to my dad for being a great father and for giving me the opportunity to live a magnificent life. To my sisters Judi & Julie: I apologize for the tough times, acknowledge the good times, and look forward to more of both. Roger Fiets: Thanks for *remaining* a special member of our family. Eric Bettelli, Co-Publisher of *Music Connection* magazine: I'm fortunate to have you as a business partner and proud to call you my friend. This book would absolutely not have been written without your support and our morning meetings. The Group: Chuck and Debbie Weiss, John Reynolds, Kim Reynolds, Gail Leone, and Arnold Greenspan. Thanks for your super support and your confidence in me and this book. Herb Tannen: Thanks for your support and your enduring friendship. Namaste! CB Brent: Thanks for being a great friend and a lifetime partner.

To a special group of friends, simply thanks for being there: Loren Cedar, Brian Leahy, Ron and Katy Fernicola, Annie Bettelli, Will, Karen, and Nicholas Seltzer, Patti Biggs, Ruben Chavez, Brad Parker, Robin Dedmon, Roxy, Joe Shultz, Rob Simbeck, Barbara Shelley, Sarah McMullen, Oscar and Nyla Arslanian, Rick Norris, Jana Waylen, Jill Merin, Griff Williams, Trish Connery, Rich Wilder.

Personal thanks to Dad's caretakers: Vida Tolman, Robert DeMarco, Melissa Page, Hillary Glikmann, Dara Stiebel, and Holly Wymore.

Personal thanks to the entire staff of *Music Connection* magazine for your commendable teamwork and your unknowing support.

Special acknowledgement to Michael Amicone for superb comma placement and excellent proofreading, and to Dave Snow for making this book look like a book.

And special thanks to the countless people who have contributed, unselfishly, to this book by sharing their personal family experiences with me.

**In loving memory of:** Jean Dolan, Fred Geis, Cliff and Jane Yarman, Joann "Annie" McNabb, Bobo, Joe Dolan, Walter Dolan, Frank Bettelli, Barbara Cedar, Mike Fernicola, Arthur Seltzer, Sue Resnik, Bert and Marie Vlaming.

**People whose teachings and writings have inspired me:** The teachers of Siddha Yoga,  Dr. Ron Smotherman, Dr. Barbara De Angelis, Dr. David Viscott, Marianne Williamson, Louise Hay, Werner Erhard, Richard Buckner, Linda Dudley, Tracy Goss, Dan Poynter, Taylor Caldwell, Sister Joanne, Billy Joel, the Beatles, Elvis Presley, Santa Claus, Jiminy Cricket,  Bugs Bunny, the Dictionary, the Encyclopedia,  Apple Macintosh.

**Author's note:** During the last days of my mother's life, we were chatting one evening in the hospital and I told her that I was preparing to teach a semester at UCLA. She responded with," What are you going to teach?" Now, my mother knew that whenever I taught at the university extension program, it was a music business course. I have no idea why she asked me that question but when I reminded her, she replied, "Why don't you teach people about THIS?"

What she was referring to was the apprehension of dying, the humbling experience of having your kids take care of you, and the strain of dealing with it all. At the time, I had no idea that it was even remotely possible for me to write a book that would teach people to deal with the problems of parent care.

This book grants one of my mother's last requests and is dedicated to my cherished memories of her.

# Part I:
# Personal

# Chapter 1

# THE FACTS SPEAK FOR THEMSELVES

*Isn't it interesting how life begins with the old caring for the young and ends with the young caring for the old.*

There is a unique phenomenon currently taking place in our society. As a result of advanced medical technology, old people are living longer, while people in their thirties and forties are having children at a "booming" rate. The result is a strenuous skirmish between your biological family and your fledgling family, both vying for your time, your emotions, and your money. It's a painful scenario that strains your relationships, alters your future and activates an annoying inner dialog which endlessly challenges your priorities:

"I'm always caught between the increasing needs of my parents and the persistent responsibilities of my own family."

"When I'm not with my parents, I'm always wondering how they are, but when I am with them, I can't wait to get home to my life."

"Why do I feel so weak when I'm around them, and so strong in other areas of my life?"

"Why do I feel so guilty all the time?"

You've heard stories about how other people are dealing with their older parents, but you never thought this would happen to you. Those once strong towers of knowledge, security, and all that you thought to be true in the world are now dependent on *your* strength and compassion. And, if all you needed was a little strength and compassion, it might be manageable. But when they become ornery and demanding, like your own children, the job of caring for them becomes extremely unfullfilling.

This book was born out of my own experience. I had just turned 41, my business was very successful, I was healthy, and my life was finally working. Then my mother passed away. It wasn't as if her death was a shock. It was expected, so I had plenty of time to get "complete" with her, to make sure she knew I loved her and that she had done a great job.

What was so unexpected, and what came as a huge shock, was that I was left with a completely new relationship with my 81-year-old father and my two adult sisters. The relationship shifted from a fun-loving, supportive, caring family to a strained relationship with a group of people that I was forced, by heritage, to interact with. What were once lengthy conversations with my sisters about my life, their life, and everyone else's life had now become short bursts of strained data regarding how dad is doing:

"Did you take care of his dinner?"

"I was with him last week, it's your turn now."

"I thought *you* paid his gas bill."

Don't get me wrong, I love my father very much, and I really wouldn't trade my sisters in for anything either. But now I realize something very important: My mother was a vital part of our family. She was the complete "caretaker" of my father — and I mean complete. My dad can hardly cook toast on his own. She was also the pivotal communicator, wherein all the news regarding my sisters and father, as well as all our other relatives, filtered through her. Without my mother acting as a buffer, we are now forced to deal with each other directly. And it's a completely different relationship, all because my sisters and I are now responsible for taking care of my father.

Previous generations handled it differently. They simply had their parent or parents move in with them. If you are comfortable with that notion, and you have the means to do it, it is a magnanimous gesture, and my hat goes off to you.

Today, technology has changed, and along with it, the care of the elderly has improved. There are a myriad of organizations that cater to the elderly, that will provide you with enough pamphlets and brochures to keep you reading for the rest of the year, as well as countless programs and senior services to keep your parent occupied while you read (see Appendix). It is even possible (and covered by most health insurance) to hire a team of experienced professionals to aid you in caring for the physical, emotional, and personal needs of your parent, so he can receive good quality help and you can be confident he is getting it. Your ultimate goal should be to take good quality care of your parent's health and well-being, and at the same time enjoy a wonderful private life of your own.

**The following facts will give you an idea of where we stand as a generation:**

• The "baby boom" generation will reach 65 between the years 2010 and 2030.

• It is estimated that you could care for your parents for the next 10 to 20 years.

• In 1988, people over 65 numbered 30.4 million and represented 12.4% of the U.S. population.

• In the United States, about 30% of all persons over age 65 live alone.

• Recent studies have shown that most U.S. families are very good at caring for their elderly; only 5% of our senior citizen population live in institutions or nursing homes.

• A recent survey of adult children who care for their parents found that 28% were under age 35, 29% were 35-49. However, 15% were over 65.

• Since 1900, the percentage of Americans over 65 has more than tripled.

• People 65 and older will represent 13% of the population by the year 2000. By the year 2025, the percentage will grow to 22%.

• In 1988, 67% of senior citizens still lived in a family situation.

• A 1988 survey revealed that the amount of people age 65-75 was eight times larger than in 1900. The amount between 75-85 was twelve times larger and the amount over 85 was 23 times larger, proving that the old are getting older.

My thanks to the National Council On Aging for providing much of the information found in this chapter.

# Chapter 2

# ABOUT YOU

*The truth is, your life comes first. That's not inconsiderate,
it's not being insensitive, it's simply the truth.*

Your parents are in a sinking rowboat, arms outstretched,
begging you for help. Your husband or wife is also in a
sinking rowboat, arms outstretched, begging you for help.
You have the opportunity to save only one. Who do you
save?

If you said, "I don't know," that would be a good answer.
Who knows what they would do if confronted by such
horrendous circumstances? But, as extreme as it sounds,
that scenario might serve as a reasonable analogy to de-
scribe the emotional "tug-of-war" that often ensues when
you are faced with the difficult responsibility of maintaining your own personal life and that of your spouse and
children, while simultaneously watching over and caring
for your aging parents. This precarious predicament can
often lead to family chaos, confusion, and emotional stress.
From the maddening inner chatter that constantly reminds
you, "They're my parents, for God's sake...I must take care

of them!" to the disparagement of actually tending to their personal, physical hygiene can be a true challenge to any adult child's character. You didn't ask for this job, you were never taught to do it, and there are few classes or seminars you can enroll in to give you the answers. You're on your own with this one, armed with only those qualities and characteristics that your parents instilled in you — honesty, integrity, pride, humility, love, etc. It could be argued that to the degree our parents taught us these qualities, to that degree they get them back.

The truth is, this is how it all turned out, and it's not going to get any better; in fact, it's going to get worse. Your parents are going to get older, weaker, and more dependent on your active participation in their lives. And according to recent longevity statistics, your current scenario could last for years, and there's nothing you can do about it!

However, there are a few things you can do to make life easier for your parents and a lot less stressful for you. But it starts with your willingness to do something that may prove to be the toughest thing you've ever had to do. Nevertheless, if you do it, it could mean the beginning of a new "stress-free" relationship with your aging parents. In order to take good care of them and still maintain your privacy and peace of mind, you must lighten the load of excess baggage you carry around with you regarding the past.

You see, there's the immediate problem of caring for your aging parents, then there's the extra junk you drag in from the past: resentment, bad memories, withheld communications, guilt, adoration, dependency, etc. This useless garbage is often more demanding and confronting than the actual care of your parents! In order to begin the process of taking stress-free/guilt-free care of them, you need to "complete" your past relationship with them and create a new one.

## Completion

The first thing you need to do to lighten the load is to get "complete" with your parents. The dictionary defines "complete" as "to bring to an end, or to conclude."

You must finally conclude and bring to an end your secret conversation that they should have raised you your way, or a different way, and if they had, things would have turned out much better. In order to be free of their domination, you must "conclude" your past with them and simply allow them to be who they are, exactly the way they are. I didn't say you had to like it, or even like them. I'm simply suggesting that, to the degree you can let go of the righteousness you've been holding on to for so long regarding who your parents are to you (and who you are to your parents), to that degree your entire relationship with them will change. You will have the capacity to care for them without the child/parent drama that keeps the "struggle" in the relationship and start interacting with them as an adult. You will have the wonderful opportunity to discover who you are without them, and when that happens, you will have your hands on the controls that will ultimately lead to taking good care of them, while still living a wonderful life of your own.

## Forgiveness

The dictionary definition of "forgive" is "to grant pardon without harboring resentment." If you really want to drop a load of excess baggage, try forgiving your parents for not being like the parents the other kids had; for not being the parents you always wanted. Harbored resentment, fear, and hatred for your parents only creates a ton of excess luggage for you and makes caring for them that much more strenuous. If you really want to minimize the stress, let go of the past. I know your reaction to this may be "Forgive THEM! After all they did to me! I'll never forgive them!" But this isn't about them, this is about you letting go of extra baggage and being, once and for all, free from the constraints of the past. And you don't need years of therapy for this one. Like the tennis shoe commercial says, "Just do it!" And here's the good news: They don't have to be there when you forgive them; in fact, they don't even have to know. You can simply forgive them in your own personal way. Perhaps a letter written to them but never sent. Oh, they'll see a change in the way you interact with them, but you do not have to make it a family announcement.

The act of forgiving goes far beyond the words "okay...I forgive you." It's in the aftermath of the words. True forgiveness creates a new foundation and a new beginning for the relationship. Every time you forgive, you wipe the slate clean; you have chosen to continue an existing relationship without the excess drama of the past — without the history. To have the opportunity to re-capture a relationship without the history is truly a gift. Imagine all the people you would re-connect with if only the history of your relationship with them could be erased. Well, the eraser is forgiveness.

Again, this isn't about your parents, it's about you. To be truly free of the inner personal battle, you must, once and for all, let go of how it used to be, how you hoped it would be, how you wished it could be, and let go of all the past child/parent junk so you can get on with the business of taking good care of yourself as well as your parents.


## Your life comes first

Did you ever notice that when you're preparing to take off in an airplane and the flight attendant is explaining the various emergency procedures, he/she always reminds you to put *your* oxygen mask on first, before you assist others? The explanation is obvious: You need to be sure that *you're* in good shape before you assist or advise anyone else.

When it comes to deciding the priority between your parents and your own family, you must realize that *your* life comes first. You need to understand this in such a way that you don't feel guilty about it. You need to accept it so clearly that you start to experience a sense of freedom with regard to the care of your parents. A sense of choice in the matter, as opposed to obligation. At first, you might think that's inconsiderate, or maybe even a little insensitive or selfish, but it's simply the truth. Your life comes first. Your life must be working in order to effectively take care of your aging parents. And don't be run by the "after all they did for me" syndrome. The care you give them must come from absolute compassion for them as your parents, not out of duty or obligation. Sure, you can be a martyr, but the emotional drama and pathos will cost you your mental stability and your physical vitality. The end result is, yes, they get taken care of, but you live a miserable life.

So let's get the priorities straight: When in doubt, *your* life comes first. That way, when you're with your parents, you can be with them 100%; and when you're with your own family, you can be with them and their needs 100%.

## A word about patience

Patience just could be the single most important "action" you can do in order to take care of your parents effectively without going bananas!

The dictionary defines "patience" as "tolerance of something or somebody over a long period of time, without complaint, but not necessarily without annoyance." Isn't that a perfect definition? Whether or not it's your parents, doesn't that just typify the exact situation you're in with *somebody* in your life? I have discovered that patience is not a thing to go out and get more of, and it's not something you can learn or get better at by practicing. Patience is simply an action that you choose to take from time to time, depending on the circumstances. Patience actually replaces complaining, elevates drama, and brings to a halt the process of adding any more input to the situation.

I say this to you because I used to go around complaining, "I don't think I have the patience for this," when in fact, I was really saying, "I really don't want to do this so I'm going to blame my quick temper, my complaining, and my overt negative actions on my lack of patience." Today, the reason I "perform" patience is absolutely a selfish one: I refuse to get crazy over the care of my parent. Or anything else, for that matter! Patience is now a tool (more like a weapon) I can use to ease my pain in the matter. Patience is the key to freedom.

**36**

You can take care of your parents with all the drama, guilt, tug-of-war, and extra baggage you want, or you can take even better care of them and have a stress-free/guilt-free relationship with them at the same time. It all starts with your willingness to perform a little patience and let go of the way it was. Whether or not your relationship with them was good or bad, whether or not your childhood was wonderful or horrendous, it's not the same today. They are not the same people physically or mentally, and you have a life and a family of your own. Your relationship with your parents must grow and mature in order for you to take care of them and still have a personal life of your own.

I know that what I'm suggesting is not easy and you may not like it. But the result is, your parents receive "drama-free," efficient care, and you still have a personal life knowing you're doing the best you can. It's up to you. They are not going to change the relationship. You must do it, or it will sadly remain the same.


**The following recommendations are designed to save your sanity and ease your stress:**

• Don't become so consumed by your parents' circumstances that you neglect your own.
• Give yourself permission to allow your life to come first.
• Forgive them for not being perfect.
• Give up trying to *prove* to them that you are a grown-up. Stop *acting* like the kid you used to be and start *interacting* with them like an adult.
• There is no reason to give in to the unreasonable demands of your parents, just as you would not do so with your children.

• After you've gone through all the quarreling, arguing, and pleading, and they still won't listen to reason, STOP. Explain to them one last time the *truth* in the matter, then let it go.

• It's okay to say no to your parents.

• You don't have to be a hero or a martyr.

• Don't add unnecessary burden to your life. Request that family members and friends take on some of the responsibility.

• Your friends always say, "I love your parents"; if so, let them help out once in a while.

• Just as this is a new and different time in *their* lives, it's also a new phase in *yours*. You must learn to accept this time in your life and simply "deal with it."

• If you are still holding on to past negative grudges or upsets regarding your parents, now is the time to let them go.

• Take an honest look at the situation. If it is beyond your control, give the job to a more qualified person and let it go. It's not worth the stress.

• Use the same philosophy that many "anonymous" groups do: "Take one day at a time."

• The "quality" of time you spend with your parents is more important than the "amount" of time. When you visit, let them know how long you will be with them and the time you must leave. Then be with them 100%.

• See them less often but stay longer, or see them more often but stay less time.

• Don't be like their generation and resist therapy. Get professional help if you need it. There are plenty of low-cost community family counseling services available.

• Take weekend trips as often as possible and get as far away from the situation as you can.

• Talk to your friends about how they care for their aging parents.

• Seek comfort from your minister, priest, rabbi, guru, etc. A strong spiritual connection may give you strength at this time.

• Talk to your parents about the strain you are going through and ask them for advice on how to deal with it.

• Be sure that the communication between your family members is open and loving. If it's not, FIX IT! The strain of taking care of your parents is enough, without the added stress of dealing with difficult family members; and chances are, *they* won't do anything about it.

• Think of yourself as your parents' coach. Help them to help themselves. The more they are able to care for themselves, the more confident and competent they become and the less pressure there is on you.

• Humor is healthy, humor is medicine, humor is sometimes the only way out. Look at the situation you have found yourself in, and from time to time, laugh at it! Have humorous conversations about the situation with your friends and family. I mean, if you really stop and think about it, the fact that your parents have become your children is hilarious!

# Chapter 3

# GUILT

*Guilt rips off your vitality,*
*challenges your self-confidence,*
*and provides no room for positive action.*

Have you ever asked yourself, "How can I treat my parents this way after all they did for me?" Do you ever feel guilty about not spending as much time with them as you could? Have you ever secretly wished your parent would just die and get it over with?

Webster defines "guilt" as "remorseful awareness of having done something wrong." The question is, what have you done wrong? Perhaps your feelings of guilt are a reaction to certain thoughts you are having that you believe to be wrong, rather than something bad you have already done. Chances are, you haven't really done anything wrong...yet, and you can't be chastised for thinking crazy thoughts, especially during this careworn time in your life.

Guilt nurtures an "I am wrong" attitude. The physical discomfort that you "feel" is a manifestation of a belief system you're stuck in called "thinking those bad thoughts is wrong." Stop believing that thinking bad thoughts is wrong. I didn't say stop thinking those thoughts, I said stop believing that you are wrong for thinking them. Your mind will wander around the most hideous places. It's been wandering since you were a kid, and it will continue to wander to even more bizarre places as an adult. It is absolutely impossible not to have bad thoughts. But so what! Have all the bad thoughts you want. You're innocent! Webster didn't define guilt as "the remorseful awareness of having *thought* something wrong."

Guilt rips off your vitality, challenges your self-confidence, and provides no room for positive action. The source of guilt in your life stems from a time in the past when you did something wrong, either yesterday or in your childhood. If you have done or said something bad to your parents and you are truly guilty, you now have an opportunity to clean it up and get on with the business of having a wonderful life. There is enough headache in your life as it is, why add extra baggage to an already heavy load?

So go ahead and have fun with all those crazy thoughts; own them, share them with a close friend, or write stories about them like Stephen King does. As long as you don't ACT on them, you are truly guilty of nothing. You're simply having strange, confused thoughts which are clearly a reaction to the uncomfortable, uncontrollable circumstances you're presently in. That's it. Lighten up! Give yourself permission to have all the insane thoughts you want, then let them pass by. To the degree you can simply have your thoughts and feelings and not become the effect of them, to that degree you will be free from the anxious feelings of guilt.

## Not-so-unusual "guilty thoughts"

- Comparing what they did for you with what you do for them; the "after all they did for me" syndrome.
- You think you are spending too much time caring for your parents and not enough with your family.
- You think you are spending too much time with your family and not enough with your parents.
- When your parent insists he/she is okay, you just let it go, even though you really think he needs help.
- You ask yourself, "How can I leave my old parent alone so much?"
- You secretly hope that some of their savings is left over for you.
- You spend time with them, then on your way home you make yourself wrong for not spending *more* time with them.
- You call them periodically, then you feel bad because you don't talk to them more often.

## The secret death wish

- When they are hard to deal with, difficult or incapacitated, you just want them to die and get it over with.
- You want them to die because they are suffering.
- You want them to die so you can get your inheritance.
- You want them to die because they are so old and feeble; you see no purpose for them to live any longer.
- They are demanding, manipulative, and mean, and you think they have lived long enough.
- You want them to have a simple, painless passing so you can finally get on with your own life.

## Predetermined guilt

"What if they die, and I haven't told them I love them?"
"What if they die, and I haven't told them I'm sorry?"
"What if they die, and I haven't said thank you?"
"What if they die right after I've had an argument with them?"

The truth is, if they die, and you haven't said or done what you wanted to, then all that means is, they died and you didn't get a chance to say or do whatever it was that you wanted to. The rest is what you add to it. Don't add drama on top of drama!

## The following recommendations should help to minimize your unnecessary feelings of guilt:

• Accept the fact that you are manifesting "guilt feelings" about imaginary scenarios in your head. Don't make yourself crazy over things that haven't happened yet. You must remain stress-free if you intend to get through this and outlive them!

• If you have done or said something bad to your parents and you are truly guilty, CLEAN IT UP! Then get on with the business of having a stress-free relationship with them.

• Express your guilt-crazed thoughts to a best friend, close relative, or a therapist.

• Don't try and avoid thinking bad thoughts. Let the bad thoughts slowly pass, while you take action on the good ones.

• In this country, you are innocent until proven guilty. Realize that you haven't done anything wrong...yet!

• When in doubt, *your* life comes first. So quit feeling so guilty about it!
• Laugh at yourself for taking it all so seriously!

# Chapter 4

# ABOUT YOUR AGING PARENTS

*They never thought this would ever happen to them.*

A close friend of mine lived across the street from an elderly couple named Doc and Nelli. They were brother and sister; Doc was 96, Nelli was over 100. Both had survived their families and had come to live together out of health and financial necessity. Being a decent person, my friend would do the neighborly thing and from time to time wave hello or strike up a friendly chat.

But as time went on, my friend noticed that Doc and Nelli really had no one to care for them, so he took it upon himself to watch over them. He would go over and make dinner, or take out the trash, or remind them to take their medicine, but most of all, he was a good, watchful companion. Doc had been a prominent dentist for many years, and in relating his life stories, my friend soon realized that Doc had once lived a very active and fulfilling life. Eventually, however, the money ran dry, and their time ran out. Nelli was committed to a community nursing home for the aged, and Doc went into the county hospital suffering from pneumonia.

One day, while my friend was visiting, Doc motioned as if he wanted to say something. He pulled my friend by the shirt, down close to him, and whispered in a distraught voice, "I never thought this would ever happen to me!"

When my friend told me this story, it really stuck with me, because the truth is, I don't get that it's ever going to happen to me. Oh, intellectually, I know that I'm going to get old and die, but I don't really "get it" like a reality. And I assert that your parents never "got it" like a reality either. Until now.

## The "squirm"

The cold reality of "*it* is happening to me" is impossible to understand until you're there living it. We manage to avoid and deny the inevitable all our lives, until the final phase of life kicks in. Then avoidance and denial no longer work as a defense mechanism and the "squirm" ensues: the absolute humiliation, embarrassment, and fear of losing control of everything and becoming an old, useless burden on people. The "squirm" is sourced in fear, validated by loss, and evidenced by anger, mood swings, depression, confusion, paranoia, dementia, hypochondria, lying, apathy, chronic complaining, unusually short temper, and disoriented and unreasonable behavior.

**At this stage of their lives, it's good to know what your parents are really afraid of:**

- Being alone
- Falling
- Forgetting
- Being penniless
- Embarrassment
- Being mugged
- Having no purpose/no longer needed by society
- Not being understood
- Being deserted by the family
- Losing their freedom
- Prolonged pain
- Losing respect
- Being dependent on a life-support system
- Being a nuisance to the family
- Dying
- Losing control

**What have they got to lose?**

The fear of losing control and freedom is statistically a big one. When you lose control, you lose the freedom to choose how you want your life to be. Older people spend much of their time trying desperately to hold on to what little they have, because, day after day, they slowly lose everything. Here are just a few of the things they are afraid of losing:
- Memory
- Physical health, hearing, eyesight, etc.
- Relatives and friends

- Normal interaction with other humans in society
- Financial security
- Independence, power, and control
- Mental stability
- Driving privileges
- Self-esteem
- Self-confidence
- Privacy
- The ability to work
- The ability to fully participate in life


## Denial

The neighbor who lives across the street from my dad called recently to inform me that he saw my father take a pretty good fall in the front yard. He said he ran over to see if he was alright, and my father insisted, "Of course I'm alright. I just tripped a little...I'll be fine." The neighbor said he was bleeding from the elbow and it didn't look too serious, but he thought he should let me know. I called my dad right away, and he denied ever falling. Then he said to me, "Don't pay any attention to those 'nosy' neighbors; they don't know what they're talking about."

This sort of cover up is common among certain people who are in denial of getting old. They resist the normal process of aging, to the degree that they place their health and well-being in jeopardy. I've watched my 81-year-old father fight his way into old age, insisting that he can still do things the way he used to and demanding that his children oblige him. It's the saddest thing I've ever seen. It's like a 12-year-old absolutely refusing to be a teenager. It's also an honest reaction to the "squirm."

### Games parents play

When it comes to control, power, and simply getting their way with you, your older parents can be as manipulative as your teenagers. The only difference is, your parents are better at it. They always win because they're your parents and you've always let them win. They've had years of practice perfecting their racket. Just because you have a life and family of your own doesn't mean you're not their little kid. They will continue to have their way with you for as long as they can. They know that all they have to do is use that all too familiar authoritative tone of voice, or weepy childish whine, and you are like putty in their hands.

### Here are just a few of the games your aging parents will play:

- They insist they are physically okay when they're obviously not.
- They insist they are not okay when they obviously are.
- They will use their age to manipulate you in order to get their way. They will passively say they are too old to do what you ask them to do, and the next day they will arrogantly insist they are still capable of handling their own affairs.
- They refuse to participate in any senior citizen discount programs or projects and insist that such activity is for old fogies.
- They act paranoid and insist that you stay with them a little longer.
- They will use their money as a bargaining piece, reminding you of all the money they have already given you, or

**51**

threaten to leave you out of the will.
- They will make guilt-laced comments: "I guess I'll have to eat alone...again."
- Sometimes it's obvious to all in the family that they cannot handle a certain chore or responsibility, but they insist they can.
- They use their grandchildren as a ploy to get favors and attention from you.


**Some hurtful but unintentional comments your parents may make:**

"You don't really care about me."
"Nobody loves me anymore."
"You are an ungrateful child."
"I just want to be left alone."
"After all I did for you."
"I'm ready to cash in my chips."
"You're never on my side."
"You'll see what it's like when you get to be my age."
" I wish I were dead."
"I don't understand why God is keeping me alive."
(You need to develop an armor for these kind of statements, because they will cut deep into your heart.)

## Some crazy things your parents may do:

- Open bank accounts with their credit cards.
- Close bank accounts.
- Constantly fire the help.
- Apply for jobs.
- Forget to eat.
- Neglect to bathe.
- Forget to feed the dog.
- Feed the dog too much.
- Forget to walk the dog.
- Walk the dog...then turn around and walk the dog again.
- Blame you for not understanding what they're trying to say or remember.
- Blame you for their life not turning out the way they had planned.

## Your parents may march to a different drummer

Just because your parents are more vulnerable does not mean you have the right to change them. If your parents have established a certain lifestyle, it is not your place to try and alter that style just because you don't think it's right. Even if their habits are a bit strange, or they do not conform to your standards, it is important that they maintain a sense of individuality to which they have been accustomed all their lives. Allowing them to be who they are will ease the tension between both of you.

## Hints to help both of you survive the "squirm":

• Honest communication is the enemy of the "squirm." Talk with your parent about these "monsters" called fear and loss. Don't deny your parent the opportunity to fully express his feelings.

• Not all older folks are at the effect of their age. Most don't like it, but some are often very content with being the age they are, mostly due to high self-confidence, an ability to participate, and an enjoyable lifestyle.

• The degree of self-confidence and self-esteem your parents have is determined by the quality of their lifestyle and their health.

• If your parents are still in good physical and mental shape, their desire to work and be active probably remains strong. In fact, the desire to contribute is usually spirited, whether or not they are physically up to it.

• Encourage and assist them in finding work or volunteer positions in their community. Expanding a favorite pasttime into a part-time money-generating enterprise could regain their self-esteem and give you peace of mind.

• Volunteer work with children or other seniors would give them a sense of pride and accomplishment.

• Sit with them and brainstorm ideas on what their interests are and what activities they would like to participate in.

• Good health is a result of continued participation.

Chapter **5**

# PURPOSE

*We humans are not interested in going for the ride*
*if there is no chance to reach for the brass ring.*

One of the most distinct human qualities we possess is our awareness of the future. We have the opportunity and the ability to plan next week, next year, or the next minute. We create the future to be a safety net that we courageously leap into with as much confidence as we can muster. The risks are high; the fall could kill us. But we humans are not interested in going for the ride if there is no chance to reach for the brass ring.

"Purpose" is conveniently located in the future. Whether you have an extraordinary grand goal, or no plan at all, purpose is inherent in all of us. The dictionary defines "purpose" as "an intended or desired result." It is your incontestable intention to survive, unless of course, you have no "reason" to survive and decide to die.

"Reason" is conveniently located in the present. The definition of "reason" is "the motive or basis for an action." You can have as much purpose and intention as you want, but if you have no reason to do it, forget it. If your father's intention is to get up in the morning and cut the grass, his reason for doing it may not be because the grass needs cutting. It may be because he simply needs to think, or to get away from you for a while.

"Purpose" is akin to survival; "reasons" are self-created. Try giving me ten purposes to run around the block. Now give me ten reasons. The truth is your parents already have an inherent purpose: to painlessly survive. What they may actually need are reasons to get up in the morning and go out and participate in life. In the past, they had a full agenda of things to do, places to go, and people to see. Their intention was to do their best to create the kind of life they dreamed about. But today, without a complete schedule of daily commitments, chores, and challenges that offer them the opportunity to really participate in life, they have to stretch to come up with enough reasons to keep the motor running. This is where you come in.

For your own peace of mind, and to enhance the quality of their old age, you can help them invent good reasons to keep on living a full life. Your old parents just want to continue to contribute, participate, and make a difference. They don't want to feel used up and finished.

**The following suggestions should pique your creative juices enough to sit down with your parents and come up with some reasons to keep them more involved in their own life, without having to invade yours:**

• Health is a result of participation. To the degree your parents are active and involved, to that degree they can remain healthy, vibrant, and autonomous.

• Give them regular "make work" to do around your house, around their house, around your office, etc.

• Hang a large calendar in a convenient location and write in their daily activities.

• Explore employment opportunities for seniors.

• Explore intern programs for seniors.

• Volunteer work could give them a sense of pride as well as an opportunity to meet new friends. Encourage your parents to volunteer for political events, charities, church functions, schools, hospitals, day-care centers, senior citizens clubs, etc.

• Explore the possibility of further education for your parents. A class or a workshop could stimulate their intellect, inspire their creativity and remind them that there is more to life than their own personal problems.

• Some community colleges and high schools offer senior education classes at little or no cost.

• Investigate the possibility of specialized senior travel services.

• Encourage them to read. Get them a library card and take them to speciality book stores. If they cannot read, there are community service programs that offer home reader services. There are also many books recorded on cassette tape.

• You *can* teach an old dog new tricks. Your parents *are* coachable and trainable.

# Chapter 6

# HANDLING A DEMANDING PARENT

*To achieve any kind of satisfactory working relationship
with your arduous, old parent, you need to be ruthless
with your actions and compassionate in your manner.*

Adult children of demanding parents often find themselves in a troubled quandary: They are committed to fulfilling the needs of their aging parents and insuring that the quality of their life is as high as possible; on the other hand, the job carries little reward. These adult children are constantly being challenged by the foolish, often useless, demands of frustrated old parents who chastise them for not living up to their expectations or accuse them of not being helpful, trustworthy children. These angry old fogies (who actually have a bounty of love for their children) are stuck in their bygone righteousness and are hopelessly out of control. They are squirming in their own fate, and they will blame everyone but themselves for it. They are not acting out of their own best interest, or yours; rather, they are "reacting" to their uncontrollable circumstances. They resist the "normal" course of "senior life" and take out their vengeance on their children, because they know nobody else would put up with such abuse. They trust no one and fear everything from doctors to dinner. They've lost the knack of friendly persuasion and replaced it with covert trickery. Their biggest upset is that they've lost control of their life. Their ability to make money, make decisions, and make you happy is outdated and defunct. They don't like being in a subservient situation any more than you like being in a caretaker roll.

However, as sad as it is to watch your parents go through this helpless time in their lives, don't get hooked by their childish, demeaning ways. Remember, your life comes first. The happier and more content your life is, the more effective you'll be in caring for them. Don't allow them to abuse you or order you around. Handle them the exact same way you handle your children. Give yourself permission to say no! It hurts sometimes, but if you know deep down inside it's for your parent's own good, you must be strong. When he/she reminds you, "I'm still your parent," agree, then stand up for yourself and do the right thing. To achieve any kind of satisfactory working relationship with your arduous, old parents you need to be ruthless with your actions and compassionate in your manner.

Ruthless compassion means that you have taken a tough stand concerning what is right, yet you are compassionate with regard to their special dilemma. Ruthless compassion is your way of loving them while doing the right thing. It gives you inherent permission to make those decisions for your parents that you know in your heart are right, even though they defy you with fierce opposition. When your parent gets too abusive, tell him/her you're not willing to communicate like this and you will leave if it continues. If the abuse does not stop, remind your parent of what you just said and tell him you will discuss it another time. Not unlike when you discipline your teenager, your parent will eventually come around.

I know you're torn between the loving memories of the person your parent was, and the hurting reality of what he has become. But you must be ruthlessly compassionate if you are to take good care of him and still maintain your own sanity. It's enough to worry and care for him, without the added stress of taking his abuse. You absolutely do not have to take his abuse. No matter what physical or mental condition he is in, you do not have to take his abuse. Stand up for yourself, and at the same time, do what you know is right for him. Your situation is special, and it takes a firm/loving hand to deal with it.

**The following recommendations are designed to help you deal with your demanding parents:**

• Upset only provokes more upset; reaction prompts more reaction. To the degree that they are insulting, you be kind. To the degree they are harsh, you be gentle. To the degree they are loud, you be quiet.

• When your parent gets too abusive, tell him/her you refuse to communicate like this and you will leave, or your parent must leave, if it continues. If the abuse does not stop, remind him of what you just said and tell him you will discuss it another time.

• Communicate with them. Encourage them to talk about this monster called losing control.

• Don't fall into the "I'm still your parent" trap. He may still be your parent, but he no longer has the right to boss you around, give you orders, or emotionally abuse you.

• Perhaps they are disappointed that their life didn't turn out the way they wanted. By abusing you, they are actually punishing themselves. Encourage them to talk about their earlier days and acknowledge them for their accomplishments.

• Get in the habit of using patience to simply allow their abusive motor to run out of gas.

• If they physically abuse you, or become violent, get professional help immediately.

• If you are verbally abused, do not react — be bigger than the abuse and let it go.

• If you are emotionally abused, seek professional help immediately.

Chapter **7**

# INTERVENTION

*Intervention is entering into your parents'
private affairs to do what is right.*

One day my father received a letter from the Department
of Motor Vehicles. He was ordered to attend a hearing to
determine whether or not he was capable of driving. This
was not a driving test. It was a hearing to determine his
mental alertness and emotional stability. He was 80-years-
old at the time.

His whole life has been about cars. Since I was a kid, he's
always had five or six cars in the yard. My dad especially
loves antique cars. His pride and joy is a 1929 Model T Ford
and a 1941 Buick convertible. He subscribes to car maga-
zines, purchases items wholesale from parts catalogs, and
once bought an antique car from a classified newspaper ad
in a city 1,000 miles away. He and my mom never agreed
on his passion for cars. She would always insist, "Why
don't you get rid of some of those damn cars?" They were
always arguing about "those damn cars." Needless to say he
never got rid of his cars, and over the years they have

become more valuable in price as well as in pride.

As he sat in the cold office of the DMV, emotionally distraught and mentally confused, it was obvious he was not capable of passing any kind of mental test, let alone drive. They revoked his license right on the spot. He was so upset that he became quiet — and my father has an Irish temper! They suggested that the only way they would reissue his license is if his doctor would recommend it. I hated them for doing this to my father, especially at this time in his life. Just a few years prior, he was forced to retire from a 50-year career in the entertainment business, and only one year ago he lost his wife of 47 years. Now they've come for his dignity.

However, as much as I hated it, I knew it was the right thing to do. I also knew it was coming. He had been in three auto accidents the previous year, all were his fault, and one seriously injured the other driver and cost our family $30,000.

About a month before my father received the DMV notice, I had a private conversation with his doctor. After a lengthy discussion regarding his mental condition, I requested that the doctor recommend to the DMV that my father not drive. He agreed wholeheartedly with this request. This was the first time in my life I had ever "intervened" in my father's personal life behind his back. My first thought was, "What am I doing? This is not my place to decide whether or not my father drives! I'm his son, his kid! I can't make a decision for my father that could strip away his last fragment of dignity and freedom!" As obvious as it was that my father was a threat to himself and others on the road, I hated that he was being stripped of his freedom — the freedom to just get in the car and go for a drive alone, anytime he wanted. And most of all, even though I knew I had done the right thing, I hated being in a position of authority over him. If it was anyone else, I would have no problem. But this was my own father!

The time to intervene in your parents' personal affairs is when their actions are a threat to themselves or others, or when they are mentally or physically incapable of performing a certain routine that they have done all their lives, like writing or depositing checks. You must determine the *right* course of action. Look at the situation carefully with other family members. Determine exactly what is wanted and needed and then provide it. You must also take into consideration how your parent would handle the situation if he/she were able. Try to make the decision the way your parent would, if given the choice.

Your parents' initial reaction to intervention is resistance. They feel and sometimes insist that they can still do it themselves. They will kick and scream as loud as your own child. They may call you names and insist that you are a selfish, ungrateful child and you're intentionally trying to torment them. As long as you have the support of the entire family and as long as you have done what you know in your heart is right, all you can do is assure your parents that what you did was a family decision made out of love, then give it time.

Whoever said "time heals all wounds" was right. There is a period of adjustment after every intervention. Patience is the key here. They will eventually come around to accept it. They may never come around to like it, but they will come around to accept it.

**The following tips may provide some helpful insights when deciding if intervention is necessary:**

• Intervention must be sourced in honesty and integrity. An intervention motivated by selfish intentions will ultimately lead to more trouble than it's worth.
• The purpose of intervention is to do what's "right" for the parent, not the adult child.
• Take an honest look at what's wanted and needed and simply provide it.
• Sometimes you can foresee the possibility of intervention in the future. The smart move is to do it now, while you have your parents' cooperation.
• Remember when you were a kid and you wanted something from your parents, you would wait until just the right moment before you asked them. Use that same manipulative technique when you intervene.
• You must take into consideration how your parent would have handled a situation if he/she were able. Try to make the decision the way your parent would if he/she had the choice.
• Consult a professional expert when invoking medical or legal interventions.
• All family members, not just one lone child, should be aware of the intervention and should be allowed to vote or give their opinion.

**Author's note:** Con their mind, not their spirit! If you and your family have attempted to intervene with little or no cooperation, then your last resort is to "con" your parents. When you are absolutely sure that intervention is the right thing, it's okay to manipulate them and, yes, even lie to them. If they are suffering from dementia or senility, or if they are completely unreasonable and unwilling to do the "right thing," then you must persuade them any way you can. Don't allow their old age, dominance, or senility to inhibit your decisions, and don't allow your "feelings" to cloud what you *know* to be the truth. Know in your heart that the honest thing to do is to be dishonest! You are the wiser now, and if you choose to take care of them, it is your responsibility to do what is right for them.

# Chapter 8

# COMMUNICATION

*We need to re-train ourselves to replace "complaining," which only provokes more upset, with "requesting," which actually invites resolve.*

Language is what separates us beasts from the rest of the pack. However, I'm not sure we are using this gift of communication to its full potential. Webster defines "communicate" as "to express oneself in such a way that one is readily and clearly understood."

Believe it or not, effective communication is an ancient concern. According to Aristotle, our communication problems stem from "a lack of clarity and an abundance of rhetoric." He went on to define "rhetoric" as "a search for all the available means of persuasion."

This probe into the manipulative use of our language may be useful in determining the reason there is such misunderstanding, sarcasm, and disdain, especially among loving family members. It seems we are more committed to selling our opinions than to achieving a mutually beneficial result. If you think about it, *everybody* has an opinion on *everything*, and for the most part, we can't wait to give ours. Webster defines "opinion" as " a judgement or appraisal formed in the mind," or "a belief less strong than positive knowledge." If you study that definition carefully, you will be reluctant to orate your opinions so hastily.

Because our precious "opinions" are at stake, we are often too quick to anticipate the response of others, and thoughtlessly too impatient to "listen." In fact, we don't listen. We simply "react." One of the most commonly used responses in the English language is "yes, but..." followed by our opinion. The result of this kind of rhetoric is chronic miscommunication, followed by anger, anxiety, and upset. In order to minimize "conversation frustration," we need to modify the way we communicate and interact with our family so that our ability to get the point across and produce the intended result is achieved with little anxiety. We need to re-train ourselves to replace "complaining," which only provokes more upset, with "requesting," which actually invites resolve.

It is important to know that in our everyday interactions with our parents and family, clear, precise communication can provide a "drama-free" solution to difficult conversations. Direct communication invites cooperation, encourages sincerity and produces a satisfactory outcome quickly.

## Experiment with the following ideas:

• Complaining provokes reaction; requesting invites resolve. Instead of complaining, try making simple requests. A request can prompt a counteroffer, a denial, or an acceptance; a complaint or an accusation inevitably invites repercussion.

• Be committed to resolving the dispute, not to winning it.
• The only thing that ultimately resolves any misunderstanding is the truth. You can argue with people all day long, but when you finally run out of verbal ammunition, it's only the truth and the facts that count.
• Don't add extra drama on top of the facts.
• Ask yourself what sort of past experience or extra baggage you're bringing to the conversation.
• Assign one person the job of communicating important family issues, i.e., if too many people speak with the doctor, you will end up with that many interpretations and conflicting reports.
• Begin to notice that most people would rather discuss the dramatic circumstances surrounding an issue, than to have any dialog regarding the facts. What most of us are sadly up to is a form of "rhetoric," as opposed to clear communication.
• The powerful pull of the drama is much greater than the simple sway of the truth.
• Common misunderstandings, such as "I thought you said..." or "I was under the impression that you meant..." are due to two things: someone not listening, or someone not telling the truth.
• The true enemy of fear is clear, honest communication.
• Communication skills can be developed at any age. You *can* teach an old dog new tricks, and your parents can be coached and trained.
• When conversing with your elderly parents speak slowly, clearly, and use as few words as possible. Avoid using long sentences to get your point across.

Chapter **9**

## SIBLINGS

*The unforeseen responsibility of caring
for your parents has the potential of ripping apart
the fabric of a once close-knit family.*

The "only child" has no choice but to care for his/her aging parents alone. Some find it a blessing, because the possibility of sibling feuding is not present to add even more pressure to an already stressful situation. Others wish they had close siblings to help carry some of the financial and time-consuming burden. But if you have brothers and sisters, you can count on at least some conflict.

The unforeseen responsibility of caring for your parents has the potential of ripping apart the fabric of a once close-knit family. Previously inseparable, loving brothers and sisters can suddenly become bitter enemies over little more than an ambivalent comment. It can create a scenario of alienation, and it can ultimately lead to a clash of egos that only serves to lessen the care of the parent and cause additional stress on the adult children.

You may be hurt because your siblings don't sympathize

or care about your personal life, or they criticize the way you interact with your parents. But, unless equitable guidelines are set and loving, cogent communication is practiced, the chance of maintaining a tight, cohesive family relationship is sadly slim.

**The following recommendations are intended to be a starting point for siblings to design an equitable plan that works for all:**

• No sibling should get off the hook. Responsibilities must be shared. Even if they live in a different state, all should share the load as equally as possible. Someone may be considered the primary care-giver, while others contribute financial, emotional, or advisory support.
• Divide responsibilities equally among siblings, according to skill level and personal preference. If one is better at shopping or another enjoys paying the bills, so be it. Make it easy on yourselves!
• Siblings may find themselves "stuck" and unable to communicate effectively with each other because of confusion, frustration, and the total intrusion of the situation on their lives. Clear, honest, straightforward dialog must be a priority between brothers and sisters in order to achieve cooperation and peace of mind.
• Communicate often, have regular meetings and phone conversations, and send each other notes and letters. Do all you can to keep a clear line of communication open.
• Know where your parent keeps important documents, i.e., bank account numbers, auto pink slips, wills & trusts, insurance policies, deeds to property, funeral plans, etc. Have one sibling be responsible for maintaining all records.

• If you're an only child, you should hire help or recruit friends and relatives. If that's not possible, contact a senior service center in your community. You, too, deserve a life independent of your parents.

• You can't force siblings to participate in the care of their parents, but you can continue to make requests of them.

**Author's note:** Two interesting phenomena began to surface as I researched this topic. Statistically, females usually carry the burden of caretaker (usually the eldest daughter). Even with regard to a married son, his wife is usually found to be the prime caretaker of his aging parents. The other interesting fact is, generally, the youngest adult sibling manages to carry the least amount of responsibility. They are usually willing to do what they are told by their older brothers or sisters, but they are rarely the source when it comes to making decisions or assigning duties.

Chapter **10**

## GRANDCHILDREN

*The notion that they have contributed
two generations to the "big picture" gives your
parents an inner sense of acknowledgement and reward.*


Your parents take full responsibility for your kids. They may not admit it, show it, or accept it, but deep down inside they know that if it weren't for them, you or your kids would not be here. So the notion that they have contributed two generations to the "big picture" gives them an inner sense of acknowledgement and reward. Go ahead, ask them!

Your children can positively enrich the life of your aging parent. If they had the opportunity, your parents would give your children even more than they gave you. The joy and excitement of interacting with their grandkids absolutely provides a sense of purpose, as well as the desire to remain healthy for as long as they can so they can continue to dance with your children!

**Here are a few suggestions to enhance the continued harmony of your three generations:**

• Don't rip off your parent or your child by not allowing them in each other's lives. If there is trouble in the family, at least allow them to communicate through the mail or by telephone.
• Be aware of manipulation, by both your child as well as your parent.
• Don't make your parents wrong or belittle them in front of their grandchildren.
• Assist your children in sending copies of their school work and audio and video tapes to their grandparents.
• Go ahead and allow your parents to spoil your kids.
• Your parents must respect the way you run your household and raise your kids. They may not agree with you, and they may fight you at every decision, but you have a right to run your life and raise your kids any way you want.

# Part II: Practical

Chapter **11**

## FAMILY BUSINESS:
## Wills, trusts, funerals, insurance
## and money

*Now is the time to learn about your parents' financial affairs.*
*Now is also the time to discuss their final wishes.*

My mother knew she was dying long before it happened
so she made certain that the family finances were in understandable, accessible order. My father was good at bringing
home the bacon, but my mother was best at saving and
investing it.

I sat with her one quiet night in the hospital, during her
final days, and she told me everything about how she took
care of all the family's financial affairs. She told me where
the bank account numbers were located, the deed to the
house, insurance papers, the living trust, and the auto pink
slips. She also told me where the envelope was that contained her burial arrangements. When she finally died, it
was, of course, an emotional time, but as far as the family
finances were concerned, it was effortless. We knew where
everything was, how everything was to be handled, and

what formalities and procedures were first priority. The family financial transition was a snap. Thanks, mom!

It's never too early to plan ahead. Now is the time to learn about your parents' financial affairs. Now is also the time to discuss their final wishes.

## The "forbidden" conversation

Arguably, the most postponed topic of conversation in history is funeral arrangements. Who wants to make plans for an unpleasant event they will have no active part in?

## The following tips should help make the conversation less confronting:

• Set up a special family meeting designed solely for the purpose of discussing the "forbidden" topic. This does not have to be a somber conversation. Celebrate the fact that the family is together doing this while everyone is still alive. Laugh about it, joke about it, and make the evening as humorous as possible.

• Who should attend the meeting? This conversation belongs to the family. It is totally up to your parents who attends, but the more family members the merrier. That way, if there is any confusion later regarding your parents' wishes, there are plenty of witnesses.

## Points that should be covered in the "forbidden" conversation:

- Where do your parents want to be buried?
- What do they want to be buried in?
- What do they want on their gravestone?
- Do they want to be cremated? If so, what shall become of the remains?
- What sort of service do they want?
- Will it be a military service?
- Would they like special friends or family members to sing, speak, or deliver a eulogy?
- Body or organ donation may be another consideration.
- Choose a funeral home and make arrangements in advance. Armed with your parents' wishes, you can make an appointment with the funeral home and finalize the plan without your parents being present. Most funeral homes bill you a few weeks after the service. A recent government ruling specifies that funeral providers must disclose the cost of all goods and services, and upon the request of the consumer must provide a written price list.
- The funeral home will request that you provide the following information: your parent's social security number, driver's license number, birthplace, maiden name, full names of his/her parents, insurance information, doctor's name, and names and birthplaces of *all* survivors and relatives. You will also be asked how many death certificates are to be ordered. My advice is to order at least 5-10 or more, depending on your parent's financial activity. In order to gain access to any insurance policies, bank accounts, deeds, auto pink slips, etc., an "original" death certificate must be presented. No one will accept a copy. The certificates are less expensive and readily available

when ordered all at the same time.

I know you've heard all this before, but hear it now straight from the horse's mouth. I'm so glad these arrangements were made for my mother before she died. All we had to do was make one phone call and *everything* was handled. It's so much better to get this business out of the way before "it" happens, than to face these decisions when you're emotionally distraught.

## Estate planning

There are attorneys who specialize in "estate planning." Hire one now! Even if your family doesn't have much, a legal "will" or, better yet, a "living trust" will save you a heck of a lot of trouble after they're gone. The initial call to an attorney costs nothing, and it's during this call that you determine your options, decide a course of action, and find out how much it will cost. Most attorneys "bill" for their services after the fact, and some will set up a payment plan with you. Remember, contact an attorney that specializes in "estate planning."

## Wills

A legally prepared will provides explicit instructions for the distribution of property and, if appropriate, how that property is to be used after a person dies. Information about burial or cremation can also be included. A will designates an individual or individuals to serve as the executor(s) responsible for carrying out the instructions of the will.

The creation of a last will and testament is a confronting

**84**

and uncomfortable action. Confronting for your parents, because it's difficult to decide how to divide the estate based on if one of them died tomorrow; uncomfortable for you because you are reluctant to encourage them to do something that is such a foreboding personal matter. But I have to tell you, it is the single most important action you can take that will assure you of a problem-free transfer of property once the inevitable happens.

Start financial planning as early as possible. Encourage your parents to meet with an attorney and create a legal "will" or "living trust." Set up the meeting yourself if they procrastinate. It is too important an issue to let slip by until it's too late. Just do it!

## The right to die — what is a living trust?

A living trust is an instrument or legal provision designed by your parents and drawn by an attorney which stipulates certain requests that are to be performed in case of their death or incapacitation while they are still living. It provides legal evidence of a person's desire not to be kept alive by artificial means should that person become terminally ill or incapacitated. Public attention is increasingly focused on "right to die" issues as advancing medical technology makes it possible to sustain, almost indefinitely, some vestige of life in dying patients. The term "right to die" refers to individual decision-making regarding the prolongation of life through the use of extreme measures. A Living Will should be discussed with the doctor and a signed copy should be added to the individual's medical file. A copy should be given to the person who will make decisions in the event that the older person is unable to do so. It should be reviewed yearly to make changes as needed.

The difference between a "living trust" and a "will" is, the contents of a "will" must be carried out by a legally appointed executor after death occurs, while the properties and requests in a "living trust" are simply transferred to the beneficiaries automatically at the time of death.

## Death benefits

Availability of death benefits should be ascertained. In some cases, these benefits could have a direct bearing on planning funeral arrangements. Death benefits may be derived from Social Security, the Veteran's Administration, life and casualty insurance, and other sources, depending upon the circumstances at the time of death. Be sure you are aware of any benefit programs your parents have committed to.

## Power of Attorney

This is a legal device which permits one individual, known as the ''principal,'' to give to another person, called the "attorney-in-fact," the authority to act on his/her behalf. The attorney-in-fact is authorized to handle banking and real estate, incur expenses, pay bills and handle a wide variety of legal affairs for a specified period of time. The Power of Attorney can continue indefinitely during the lifetime of the principal so long as that person is competent and capable of granting Power of Attorney. If the principal becomes comatose or mentally incompetent, the Power of

Attorney automatically expires, just as it would if the principal dies. Therefore, this Power of Attorney may expire just when it is most needed.

## Durable Power of Attorney

Because Power of Attorney is limited by competency of the principal, some states have authorized a special legal device for the principal to express intent concerning the durability of the Power of Attorney to survive disability or incompetency. This legal device is an important alternative to guardianship, conservatorship, or trusteeship. The laws vary from state to state, and since this puts a considerable amount of power in the hands of the attorney-in-fact, it should be drawn up by an attorney licensed to practice in the state of the client. This device is to compensate for the period of time when an individual becomes incompetent to manage his/her own affairs properly.

## Guardianship

Guardianship or conservatorship is a legal mechanism by which the court declares a person incompetent and appoints a guardian. The court transfers the responsibility for managing financial affairs, living arrangements, and medical care decisions to the guardian.

## Social Security

Social Security is a national retirement income supplement available to nine out of ten Americans over age 65 (persons age 62 may qualify under certain conditions). Monthly benefits are available to workers upon retirement, to their dependents and/or survivors, and to the severely disabled. Spouses and widows/widowers may be eligible for special benefits, including death benefits. Individuals who are disabled before 65 may also apply for Social Security disability benefits. Older persons may have their Social Security checks sent directly to their bank by the United States Government. This prevents lost or stolen checks and eliminates a trip to the bank to deposit the check. Individuals who wish to apply for Social Security may write or telephone their local Social Security office for instructions on how to file a claim.

## Supplemental Security Income (SSI)

Supplemental Security Income (SSI) assures a minimum monthly income to needy persons with limited income and resources, who are 65, blind or disabled. Eligibility is based on income and assets. Ask your local Social Security office for information regarding this program.

## Tax benefits

There are a variety of federal, state or local tax benefits available to older persons. Contact the Internal Revenue Service, or state and local tax offices for further information. Also, property tax exemptions and/or deferrals are available in some communities to persons over 65 who have a limited income. Contact the local tax office for more information.

## Home Equity Conversion

Home equity conversion is a program which enables the owner to utilize the equity in a home for purchase of needed services. Some banks participate in this type of program and will arrange to free up these often-overlooked resources to help cover the costs of services needed by your older parent. Ask a loan officer at your bank for information on this program.

## Medicare

Medicare is a federal health insurance program which helps defray many of the medical expenses of most Americans over the age of 65. Medicare will pay for many health care services, but not all of them. Medicare does not cover custodial care or care that is not determined to be reasonable and necessary for the diagnosis or treatment of an illness or injury. In some instances, Medicare may pay for certain psychiatric services. It is possible to privately purchase supplemental health insurance. This is sometimes referred to as "Medigap." Before purchasing a policy, care should be taken to assure that the plan provides the coverage that your parent wants and needs.

Medicare has two parts: Part "A" Hospital Insurance, and Part "B" Medical Insurance. Part "A" helps pay the cost

**89**

of inpatient hospital care. In some instances, Part "A" helps pay for home health care, inpatient care in a skilled nursing facility, and hospice care. Part B helps pay for medically necessary doctors' services, outpatient hospital services and some other medical services. Enrollees must pay a monthly premium for Part B.

Your parent should apply for Medicare benefits three months prior to his/her 65th birthday. Detailed information about Medicare benefits, including a number of pamphlets explaining coverage, can be obtained from your local Social Security office.

## Medicaid

Medicaid is a health care program for low-income persons cooperatively financed by federal and state governments. Administered by states, the program provides for medical services to eligible individuals. Benefits cover both institutional and outpatient services. However, the types of services covered may differ from state to state. Each state has a set of criteria which establishes eligibility for services under this program. Further information about Medicaid is available at your county welfare, health, or social service departments.

## MONEY: Their life savings or your inheritance

You can't deny the fact that the subject of "money" is often the most confrontive issue regarding the care of your parents. It can cause jealousy and resentment among loving siblings, greedy tendencies in the most unlikely child, and threaten the continued health and welfare of your parents. It affects both their well-being and your inheritance. Its powerful influence can insure the quality of their limited future, or guarantee you a down payment on a new home.

The most important thing to remember is that their life savings is simply that: THEIR LIFE SAVINGS! It's their money first. If you have to spend every last dime of your inheritance taking care of them, that's the breaks. Marry somebody rich!

**The following recommendations should benefit your parents, but ultimately, they will free you from the worry of how efficiently the family business affairs are being handled:**

• The time to begin the process of taking over your parents' financial and business affairs is when you begin to notice that the job becomes a burden to them, or when you have to intervene because they are making repeated mistakes. Determine your parents' current financial situation, including income and expenses, and create a simple budget.
• When you think it's time to intervene, have their bills sent to you, along with their income checks.
• Consult a tax expert for any special tax benefits for senior citizens.
• Know their account numbers, driver's license number, social security numbers, credit card numbers, insurance policy information, stocks, property investments, auto pink slips, etc.
• Your parents must apply for Social Security in order for it to become active.

• Assist your parents in carefully choosing professional legal help.

• Do not write up a "do-it-yourself" will.

• Investigate the possibility of a "living trust" with your parents and an attorney who specializes in "estate planning."

• Issues concerning property, estates, and trusts are governed by state laws and, in some cases, local ordinances. If finances do not permit hiring a private attorney, there are programs that provide both legal advice and legal representation in court to elderly and low-income persons. For information, contact the local Bar Association or your local Agency on Aging.

• Sometimes, tenant/landlord issues arise regarding leases, services, rental rights, and obligations. To get advice, contact your landlord tenant advisory council, a lawyer, or your local Agency on Aging.

My thanks to the U.S. Department Of Health And Human Services for providing many of the facts contained in this chapter. I suggest you contact them for additional information (see Appendix).

Chapter **12**

## HOW TO BUILD A SUPPORT TEAM

*There is absolutely no reason you should
have to care for your aging parents alone.*

Previous generations had little choice when it came to caring for their elderly parents. Much of the care was for unknown physical ailments, and the lack of proper insurance usually wiped out the family savings. The alternatives were to move them in, or place them in a home for the aged.

Today, the options have increased. Thanks to Medicare, Medicaid, extensive senior community services, and modern technology, there is absolutely no reason you should have to care for your aging parents alone.

The father of a close friend of mine is bedridden, due to a variety of physical malfunctions. My friend is an only child and lives 300 miles away from his dad — it is impossible for either of them to move closer at this time. The following support team was created to care for his father:

**Home aid:** .......................................covered by Medicare
Four days a week. Bathe, shave, shampoo, etc.

**Physical therapy:** ...........................covered by Medicare
Three times a week. Work his legs, massage his muscles, assist him in walking and getting exercise.

**Registered nurse:** ...........................covered by Medicare
Daily. Check all vital signs, including blood pressure, weight, breathing, pulse, etc.

**Kidney dialysis:** .............................covered by Medicare
Three days a week in his home.

**Night-sitter:** ..........................................................$70 a day
Seven days a week. Responsible for tending to any and all nightly needs, from a glass of water to an empty bed pan.

**Regular doctor visit:** .....................covered by Medicare
Every three weeks.

Including his wife and his son, there is a team of eight people caring for my friend's father, and the only extra money being spent is the night-sitter, at $70 a day.

**The following list of "at-home" services should be helpful in customizing a support team for your parent. Most communities have an Area Agency on Aging whose primary function is to provide people with information about where to go for help in caring for the elderly. Also, contact the "senior social services" department in your community, or check the "help wanted" section of your local newspaper:**

**Visiting nurses:** If your parent is suffering from a chronic disease or recovering from a serious illness, a registered nurse will regularly observe all vital signs, check blood pressure, breathing, pulse, dress bandages, administer medication and injections, provide catheter care, and other skilled nursing services.

**Senior day care services:** These services include light housekeeping, personal errands, grocery shopping, meal preparation, companionship, social outings, etc.

**Home aid:** This service is designed to make your parent look and feel good. Services include bathing, manicures and pedicures, light massage, hairstyling, etc.

**Physical therapy:** A licensed therapist will manipulate and stimulate your parent's legs, arms and muscles and assist him/her in getting proper exercise.

**24-hour phone in service:** This service provides you with peace of mind, in case your parent falls or is incapacitated and can't call for help. Volunteers phone your parent at a predetermined time every day. If he fails to answer, a specific action is taken. Also, the U.S. Post Office offers ''Carrier Alert'' Services which keeps an eye on the frequency of your parent's mail pick-up.

**Night-sitter:** This paid assistant will spend the night at your parent's home and provide whatever care or assistance is needed.

**Volunteer visitors:** Some colleges may provide this service free as extra credit for their sociology students. The volunteer visits your parent on a regular basis, for 2 to 3 hours once each week, and allows your parent to tell all the stories you've heard a million times, in addition to renting movies, playing board games, and providing companionship.

**Meals on Wheels:** This volunteer service (or one similar)

95

is found in many communities around the country. The service provides a nutritious meal delivered daily at little or no cost.

**Handyman service:** General home repairs—from leaky plumbing to burnt-out light bulbs. The service also includes yard care, snow removal, and exterior home repair. Limited home improvement grants and/or loans are available to older persons who meet income eligibility guidelines under a federal block grant program. Funds can be used for roofing, ramps, insulation, etc.

**Social/recreational activities:** Many communities support group activities for social, physical, religious, and recreational purposes. Senior Centers offer a good opportunity for recreation and social involvement with others. There are a number of other groups that focus on special interests such as arts and crafts, education, and travel. Contact the senior community center in your area.

**Transportation:** If your parent doesn't drive, and public transportation is inconvenient or not available, you could hire someone to drive him wherever he needs to go, including the doctor, market, bank, library, senior community center, a friend's home, etc. Taxi companies usually provide discount rates to seniors — notify the driver in advance if your parent needs any assistance getting in and out of the vehicle. A number of communities offer free or low-cost door-to-door transportation services for older persons such as vans or mini-buses which accommodate wheelchairs, walkers, and other devices. Transportation may be provided to and from the doctor's office, grocery store, pharmacy, and other essential errands.

**Medical equipment:** When ordered by a physician, rental or purchase of medical equipment is covered by Medicare or Medicaid. Some communities supply medical equipment through local voluntary agencies. In addition to your local Area Agency on Aging, ask your local health department for information.

**Support groups:** Groups have been formed in many communities which provide information and emotional support to older persons and/or their caregivers. These groups frequently focus on special needs such as Alzheimer's disease, terminally ill persons, bereavement, and other serious life situations. Ask your local Area Agency on Aging for information.

**Respite care:** There are ways that a relative can be relieved of caregiving duties for a short period of time. Some communities offer volunteer or paid "respite care," which provides temporary care for an impaired older person so that the family members who provide daily care can have some time off.

**The Older Americans Act:** There are a variety of services funded by the Older Americans Act, which are available in most communities. These services include information and referral, homemaker/home health aides, transportation, congregate and home-delivered meals, and other supportive services. Contributions are encouraged; however, there is no fee for services under the Older Americans Act. The types of services available vary in each community based upon the needs and resources of a given locality. Contact your local Area Agency on Aging for information about obtaining these services.

## Reminders

• Take advantage of the services provided by Medicare and the senior centers in your community and create your own support team for your parent. Work with your parent's doctor to determine what care is actually wanted and needed.
• Divide responsibilities among your willing friends and family. Set it up so that no one really goes out of his/her way. Make it easy for the whole team.
• Check into any "senior companion" programs in your parent's community.
• Take advantage of home-delivered meals, such as "Meals on Wheels," and any other homemaker services as the need increases.
• Assist your parent in gathering any information regarding associations, clubs, and organizations for seniors in his/her area.
• Hire a part-time college student or retired person to help you care for your parent.

My thanks to the U.S. Department Of Health And Human Services for providing many of the facts contained in this chapter. I suggest you contact them for additional information (see Appendix).

# Chapter 13

# WHERE SHOULD THEY LIVE?

*"...Will you still need me,*
*will you still feed me,*
*when I'm sixty-four?"*

This is a family conversation, and it's a tough one. The more siblings, the more opinions...the more options, the more decisions...the more choices, the more arguments. Determine what lifestyle your parent is accustomed to and try to keep in as much of his/her usual routine as possible. But, keep in mind, the commitment must be on the quality of life for both you and your parent, not just your parent. Never make "dramatic" decisions based on your feelings or emotions, and never, never invite your parent to live with you out of guilt. To the degree you can stay focused on the commitment and keep the guilt and drama out of the conversation, to that degree you and your family will be able to make a clear choice of where your parent will spend his remaining years. Fortunately, the options are limited to only a few, therefore the choices are already narrowed down:

1) Your parent lives alone, with or without a support team.
2) He lives with a family member or a roommate.
3) He lives in a nursing home or retirement complex.

The following three chapters address these choices....

# Chapter 14

# PARENTS THAT LIVE ALONE

*Guarantee your parent's safety, maintain*
*his mobility, and stay in communication.*
*Your parent will be safe and warm, and you'll sleep at night!*

The National Center For Health Services recently stated that most older people who live alone have at least one child living nearby. In fact, 78% of single Americans over age 85 live near at least one of their children.

69% of parents between the ages of 65-74 live near a child.

70% of parents between the ages of 75-84 live near a child.

78% of parents over age 85 live near a child.

## Advantages to living alone:

- Your parent makes the decisions for himself and can live life the way he chooses.
- His own home provides him with a sense of privacy,

independence and self-worth.
- Your parent is able to maintain a sense of individual spirit and personality.
- He remains proud and self-governing.
- Those who survive the longest alone are the ones that participate the most in life, i.e., friends, community involvement, social outings, hobbies, etc.


## Disadvantages of living alone:

Your parent may not be able to take care of himself effectively. Ask yourself these questions:
- Is your parent willing/able to continue to be independent?
- Is he/she physically and mentally capable of living alone?
- Is he financially independent?
- Are you financially prepared to assist him?
- Can he administer his own medication properly?
- Is he able to prepare nutritious meals for himself?
- Is he able to care for his own personal hygiene properly?
- Can he/she handle all the small and large appliances in the kitchen?
- Can he perform light housekeeping chores like changing the sheets, doing the laundry, cleaning the bathroom, etc.?
- Does he live in a safe neighborhood?
- Does he have enough friends and family nearby to help combat loneliness?
- Will he be able to keep track of important documents, appointments, etc.?
- Is his house safe from cold, heat, fire, intruders, etc.?

**Safety, mobility and loneliness are the three most critical factors to take into consideration when your parent lives alone. The following recommendations should help provide a few guidelines:**

## Safety

• Parent-proof your parent's home.
• Check into the possibility of installing banisters and guard rails in various locations inside and outside the house; don't forget a bathtub guard rail.
• Hide spare sets of keys, both inside and outside the house, so that *you* know where they are.
• Install dead-bolt locks on all doors.
• Install night lights and timers.
• Remove all loose rugs from the interior and exterior of the house.
• Inform the police that your parent lives alone and request that they occasionally drive by. Also, request that they do a safety/security check of his home.
• Have the local utility companies do a complete check of the property for leaks and improvements and make energy-saving suggestions.
• Have the fire department pay a visit to inspect for fire hazards.
• Create an emergency plan in case of earthquake, hurricane, tornados, power outages, gas leaks, etc.
• List important phone numbers in large writing next to every phone.
• Be sure you exchange phone numbers with a neighbor, and that the neighbor knows what your parent's condition is. Pay or reward the neighbor to keep a regular eye on your parent.

**103**

• Create a checklist before your parent goes to bed that includes:
- ❑ Turn off gas.
- ❑ Turn off lights.
- ❑ Running water.
- ❑ Lock all doors and windows.
- ❑ Walk the dog.
- ❑ Take medicine, etc.

## Mobility

• Be sure your parent gets out into the world often enough.
• Research *all* transportation options and schedules in your parent's community.
• Most taxi companies offer discount rates to seniors.
• If your parent is disabled or has a communication problem, call the taxi company ahead of time and let them know the details of the trip — destination, times, if your parent requires assistance getting in and out of the vehicle, etc.
• Talk to a neighbor about the possibility of driving your parent on short errands.
• Hire a college student to drive your parent.

## Loneliness

• Call your parent at the same time every day or week. He will begin to look forward to the call and make plans to tell you what's been happening in his life.
• Have a large note pad next to his phone, and when he thinks of things to tell you, have him write it on the pad.
• Pay a neighbor dinner and movie expenses to take your

parent out once a week.
• Instruct your parent on the use of a video tape machine; buy or rent his/her favorite movies.
• Request that every member of the family phone and visit regularly.
• Remind your parent's friends to phone and visit often.
• Hire a day-time companion.
• Contact your local college and ask if they provide a "volunteer visitor" program for the senior community.

# Chapter 15

# IF THEY LIVE WITH YOU

*If everyone who lives in the house shows
a willingness to cooperate, this can be an
extremely joyous and rewarding experience.*

My grandfather "Bobo" lived with us until I was twelve...then he died. From the moment I was aware of him to the day he died, we were extremely close, and he was a special part of my childhood. My parents were cautious not to show any animosity regarding his living with us, and I never heard them argue about him once. As far as I was concerned, this was the way life was — I actually felt like I had it better than the other kids because my grandfather lived with me!

A three-generation household can be a wonderful experience for some and a confronting situation for others. The decision to move your parent in with you should be made only after everyone in the family has had the opportunity to express their point of view. There should be no martyrs here. The individual needs of each person must be considered, and the rights of each person must be respected. The right to privacy, the right to include friends, TV privileges, kitchen privileges, etc., are topics that should be included in the initial conversation. If everyone who lives in the house shows a willingness to cooperate, this can be an extremely joyous and rewarding experience.

### Advantages of having your parent live with you:

- Someone is constantly watching over your parent's well-being.
- Most, if not all, of your parent's survival needs are met.
- Your parent has a constant supply of conversation and companionship.
- Live-in grandparents can be a great source of companionship to kids.
- Your parent may contribute financially to the rent, mortgage payment, food, etc.
- Your parent could share household responsibilities, including cooking, yard work, laundry, etc.
- Allowing your parent to participate in your life could give both of you a rich experience.

### Disadvantages of having your parent live with you:

- It can be an incredible intrusion on your privacy, as well as a humbling experience for your parent.
- The responsibilities of a three-generation household can be enormous.
- Chances are, whatever past relationship you had with your parent will be brought back into your life.

- The financial demands may be greater than you expected.
- There is no time or place to be alone with your friends and family.
- Simple food preparation for a three-generation family can be a frustrating challenge.
- The demands of your parent's transportation needs could challenge your daily schedule.
- Your intention to have your parent live with you was good, but if it doesn't work out, asking him to leave could result in a major family upheaval.

## Clear communication is most important

At a family meeting, discuss what is wanted and needed by each member of the family. Allocate various household responsibilities and decide what sacrifices will be made. Address these topics at the meeting:

❏ Are all the members of your family willing to have another person live in the house?

❏ Do your spouse and children realize their added responsibilities when a grandparent moves in with them?

❏ Who sleeps where? Will your parent have his/her own room? How will that affect other members of the family?

❏ Is there sufficient space to provide everyone in the house with enough privacy?

❏ Will your parent be a prisoner in your home without the benefit of having his friends over?

❏ When you have dinner parties or when friends casually drop in, will your parent be invited to participate?

❏ If anyone in the family wants "private time," will that offend anyone else?

❏ Most grandparents make exceptional baby-sitters, but is

baby-sitting a requirement to live in your home?

❑ Simple food preparation for a three-generation family can turn out to be a major event. How will it work in your house?

❑ The demands of your parent's transportation needs could challenge your daily schedule. Be sure that the subject of transportation is discussed and all possible scenarios are examined.

❑ Discuss the possibility of a six-month trial period.

❑ Create the rules of the house and post them on a family bulletin board.

❑ Just so you know, it is common for parents to contribute financially in exchange for living with you.


## OPTIONS:

**Echo housing and mobile homes:** Echo housing or "grannie flats" are usually small living units in the back or side yards of a single family home. A mobile home can offer many of the same advantages. However, in both cases, zoning restrictions may prohibit such an arrangement in urban areas.

**Shared housing:** Shared housing is a living arrangement in which two or more unrelated individuals share the common areas of a house or apartment while maintaining their own private space, such as a bedroom. In home matching programs, potential home or apartment sharers are introduced to each other.

A shared housing arrangement has three primary benefits:

1) Financial benefits are derived from pooling resources to pay the rent, utilities, and other expenses associated with maintaining a home.

2) Sharing the responsibility of homemaking chores with others.

3) Social interaction with other residents.

Check your local newspaper or senior community center for an agency which specializes in senior shared housing.

My thanks to the U.S. Department Of Health And Human Services for providing many of the facts contained in this chapter. I suggest you contact them for additional information (see Appendix).

Chapter **16**

# NURSING HOMES AND
# RETIREMENT COMMUNITIES

*Your first reaction to a nursing home
may be very disheartening:
You can't imagine anyone living in a place
like this, let alone your parent.*

The purpose of a nursing home is to provide long-term
care for elderly people who are too sick or too feeble to care
for themselves or do not have any family or friends that are
able to care for them. The decision to place your parent in
a nursing home must be discussed thoroughly by all family
members as well as your parent. However, once the decision is reached, you are faced with a variety of new
questions to be answered. The following information should
provide some insight on the subject.

## Basic facts

The federal government has classified nursing institutions into three categories:

1) Skilled Nursing Facility: Must provide 24-hour supervision by a staff of skilled nurses assisted by physicians.

2) Intermediate Care Facility: For patients who do not require highly skilled medical treatment.

3) Extended Care Facility: Provides custodial care only; no medically skilled professionals.

- About 25,000 nursing homes operate nationally.

- There are approximately 1.5 million persons living in nursing homes; 85% are over 65.

- Various federal programs fund over half the cost of nursing home care; Medicaid is the primary provider.

- Some facilities are especially designed for "private-pay" patients.

- Federal and state agencies set the standards regulating quality of care, as well as levels of professional skills required for most nursing homes.

- The U.S. Department of Health and Human Services requires that nursing homes assure their patients certain rights, including privacy, visitation, regular medical and dental exams, etc.

## Your parent has rights

A person entering a nursing home continues to have the same civil and property rights he/she had before entering the home. Nursing homes participating in the Medicaid and Medicare programs must have established patients' rights policies. Ask the nursing home for a copy of its patients' rights policies. Contact the Nursing Home Ombudsman program for more information. The Ombudsman can be reached through your State Agency on Aging.

## Nursing Home Ombudsman

After your parent is comfortably placed in a home, if a question or problem arises regarding care or treatment, the first step in resolving the issue is to talk to the nursing staff or the social worker. If the issue continues to be of concern, the next step is to talk to the nursing home administrator. If these steps do not resolve the issue, the resident and/or the family may want to contact the Nursing Home Ombudsman who serves the community. The Ombudsman works with nursing home residents and families to negotiate a satisfactory resolution to questions and/or problems which have surfaced. All states and many local communities have an Ombudsman who is responsible for investigating and resolving complaints made by or on behalf of residents in long-term care facilities. The Ombudsman monitors the implementation of federal, state and local laws governing long-term care facilities. In many areas, the Ombudsman sponsors and encourages the development of local citizen groups to promote quality care in long-term care facilities.

## Advantages of a nursing home:

- You are assured that your parent is getting the best care possible.
- Your parent has all of his survival needs met.
- He can associate with people his own age.
- Your parent can involve himself in a variety of social activities.
- Moving to a new environment is like starting over. It could give your parent a renewed vigor for life.

## Disadvantages of a nursing home:

- You are never really confident that your parent is getting the best care.
- Your parent could lose his willingness to continue living.
- You may regret the decision later.
- You may have to explain the situation over and over, and your parent still may not understand why you put him in a home.
- He may accuse you of abandoning him.
- He may become frightened that he is going to die alone in a cold, uncaring place.
- Nursing homes are viewed as the final resting place, before the actual final resting place.


## Finding the right home for your parent

Friends, doctors, social workers, hospital staff, and clergy are the best sources of information when looking for a good nursing home. There are three primary factors to consider when choosing a nursing home:

1) Type of care required: Discuss your parent's condition with his/her physician and other family members. Talk to everyone that knows your parent and get an honest profile of your parent's mental and physical condition. Questions regarding the type of care that may be required should be discussed with your parent's doctor.

2) Finances: Make a realistic analysis of your parent's financial status. There should be a complete inventory of available resources. This includes source and level of income, property, savings accounts, stocks and bonds, veteran's benefits, pension provisions, insurance benefits,

and any family assistance available. If your parent can't afford to pay, the choice of a nursing home is limited to a facility which accepts Medicaid and has an opening. Local social services departments in your community will provide information about eligibility requirements and procedures for applying for assistance from publicly financed programs.

3) Location: Obviously, the best geographic location is a facility which is most convenient to family and friends.

## When searching for a quality nursing home, design a checklist that includes the following:

❑ Medication control
❑ 24-hr. attendant
❑ Physician, psychiatrist, podiatrist on the premises
❑ Shuttle transportation
❑ 24-hour visiting rights
❑ Emergency buttons in the room
❑ Special diet accommodations
❑ Walking distance from parks, shopping malls, churches, theaters, etc.
❑ Spacious rooms with private baths
❑ Nutritious meals
❑ Friendly staff
❑ Clean, freshly painted, and kept-up rooms
❑ Recreational and cultural programs
❑ Religious services
❑ State-licensed facility
❑ Make a surprise visit to the home during peak hours. Talk to the staff as well as the people that live there. Get an honest sense if your parent would be satisified there.

## Emergency placement

Many people delay or avoid discussions and decisions about nursing home placement until failing health forces an immediate decision. If immediate help is needed in locating a nursing home or determining the quality of care provided in a particular facility, contact your Area Agency on Aging for assistance. Additional information can be obtained through your parent's physician, local senior center, Social Security office, community hospitals, and clergy. Even though the need for nursing home placement is urgent, it is still essential to consider the type of care needed, the finances available, and the convenience of the facility's location.

## How to handle your parent's reaction:

• Tell your parent the truth every step of the way.
• When your parent makes comments like "how can you put me in a place like this?" continually assure him that the decision is a family one made out of love.
• Convince him you understand his fear and anxiety. Assure him that you and other friends and family will call or visit and he is not being abandoned or forgotten.
• The best way for you to assure quality care for your parent in a nursing home is to encourage your family to remain involved with your parent through frequent visiting and good communication with the nursing home staff.
• When you start to think "how can I do this to my own parent?" go ahead and have the thought, then let it pass. I guarantee you will have the thought. I can also guarantee that it will pass.

**118**

## Educate yourself

Research every aspect of a nursing home and request information from government agencies and community senior centers. Understand your parent's rights, your rights, the benefits, the disadvantages, and the financial commitment. Your first reaction to a nursing home may be very disheartening — you can't imagine anyone living in a place like this, let alone your parent. Try to look beyond the generic starkness of the place. Thoroughly check out each facility for all it has to offer first, then consider the down side.

Try to anticipate ahead of time if your parent will need nursing home care. Early planning allows time for full exploration of the options available and will improve the chances of making appropriate decisions at the most appropriate time.


## OPTIONS:

**Retirement and life-care communities:** There are a variety of retirement and life-care communities available in different parts of the country. Many retirement communities offer single family dwellings, rental apartments, condominiums, and cooperatives which are sold or rented in the usual manner. In some parts of the country, living arrangements referred to as "life-care communities" are available. In these communities, the resident, upon application, makes a one-time payment and agrees to pay a monthly fee for services provided. Many of these facilities have a "graduated care" arrangement which permits the resident to move from his/her own apartment into a nursing home

**119**

unit, which includes skilled nursing home care, if needed. Frequently, these units will arrange for basic medical services. State and local regulations and requirements governing the operation and financing of these facilities vary considerably. Some states have no regulations or requirements regarding such facilities, while other states prohibit the development of such facilities.

Facilities which are well-designed and carefully administered offer comfortable and independent living to many older people. In all instances, if a family is considering this as a desirable housing alternative, an on-site visit to the facility and careful checking into the financial solvency of the organization is a must. Obviously, before entering into any contractual arrangements with such a facility, an attorney should be consulted.

**Congregate and senior housing (apartments):** Congregate and group living arrangements are available for rental to older people in many communities. Some facilities are privately financed, and others are publicly assisted. In those communities which have congregate living facilities for low- income older people, application for a subsidized rental unit is made through the local Housing Authority.

**Accessory apartments:** An accessory apartment is an independent living unit with its own outside entrance, kitchen, and bath. Accessory apartments may be especially desirable for younger families who want their older relative(s) near, or for older residents of large houses with space that could be converted into an accessory apartment.

My thanks to the U.S. Department Of Health And Human Services for providing many of the facts contained

**120**

in this chapter. I suggest you contact them for additional information (see Appendix).

# Chapter 17

# LONG-DISTANCE CARE

*Love has no borders or boundaries.*

After interviewing numerous people on the subject of long-distance parent care, I found an inventory of diverse opinion. Some people who live far away from their needing parent feel lucky that they're off the hook and relieved that they don't have to take on the responsibility. Either they have other siblings or friends taking good care of their parent, or the relationship with their parent is unfriendly or apathetic and caring for him/her is not a priority. Others feel ashamed that they are not in a financial position to live near their parent, or at least move him closer. Still others are in a constant state of worry and anxiety regarding the quality of care their parent is getting in their absence. They hear sporadic stories of their parent falling or having trouble walking or not eating or reports that he is depressed and not doing so well. So much so that one person told me, "Every time my phone rings, it's like a jolt to my nervous system...I just know it's bad news about my mother."

One of the most commonly shared dilemmas regarding

the long-distance care of a parent is the feeling of being out of control — helpless when your parent is in trouble and you cannot be there to assist, concerned about matters that you have no power over. And you just know that if your parent lived closer, he would receive much better care. For some, it even gets to the point that they leave their own family behind, book a flight or drive long distances on a "hunch" or a "feeling" that their parent needs them, only to find their parent doing just fine. If these adult children cry wolf too many times, their own family starts to question their stability.

Then there's the confronting debate of allowing others to care for your parent. Whether they're siblings or friends, there is a dangerous tendency to dictate your point of view over the phone, or worse yet, blame them or make them wrong for not caring for your parent the way you would if you were there. However, the inevitable response to that sort of accusation is "it's easy for you to dictate orders when you're a 1,000 miles away," or "you're not here to handle the day-to-day chores or decisions so you really don't understand what's going on here!"

Anyway you look at it, trying to care for your parent long distance and still live a stress-free life of your own can be a challenging dilemma.

**The following suggestions are designed to reduce your worrying and increase your confidence so that you feel assured your parent is getting the best care possible:**

• Encourage all family members to call your parent at least once each week.

• Communicate with your parent by using cassettes, video, fax, etc.

• Clear communication is critical when it comes to long-distance care. When you speak to the people who are caring for your parent, keep the conversation focused and away from the drama.

• Make friends with your parent's neighbors and request that they stay in touch with your parent on a regular basis.

• Visit your parent as often as possible. Whenever you come to town, throw a party or a dinner and invite the entire support team you've set up.

• Communicate with your parent's clergy and encourage them to occasionally look in on your parent.

• Don't underestimate the power of acknowledgement. From time to time, send a card, flowers, a thank you note, or a small gift to the people who care for your parent. Don't forget to include them on your holiday greeting card mailing list. Assure them that you will reimburse them for any money they spend on your parent.

• When your parent lives far away, it can be very difficult for you to give up control and allow others to care for him. But if you have no choice...GIVE IT UP! Let others do it. Don't make yourself crazy. See to it that your parent is getting the best care possible, then let it go!

Chapter **18**

# DOCTORS

*Clear, honest, "no drama" communication is a key factor in developing a straightforward dialog with medical personnel.*

There is a phenomenon that takes place whenever we talk to doctors: We simply believe them; they say it, and we hold it as law. It's like when we read a magazine or a newspaper: As long as it has justified margins and a bold headline, we simply believe it.

Now I realize that doctors went to school for a long time and studied long hours and stressed themselves out taking all those exams and finals, and I have the greatest respect for their scholastic tenacity and commitment to the profession. But whoever said "get a second opinion" was probably at the top of his class. The reason you get a second opinion is because the person who gave you the first one could be wrong. It's just like the stock market: You buy a certain stock based on the professional, expert advice of your stockbroker that it's probably going up. Now you must realize that someone is going to sell that same stock based on the expert, professional, educated advice of *their* stockbroker that it's probably going down. Both buyer and seller were advised by expert, educated professionals.

Alternative medical opinions are not simply for the patient. Knowing that the determined diagnosis, as well as the resulting prognosis, is founded in strong factual evidence gives you a sense of trust and confidence (as well as relief) that the best care is being administered to your parent.

My mother's final stint in the hospital lasted three months. She had heart disease, and during that time we actually got third and fourth opinions. It was also during this time that I acquired a real education in how to communicate with doctors. In the beginning, they were giving me and my sister quick medical narrative on the extremely critical condition of our mother. That wasn't good enough for us. We decided that if mom was going to die, we wanted the quality of her remaining time to be high and her degree of pain and suffering to be low. We were willing to do anything to achieve that result so we began by shifting the way we communicated with the doctors and nurses. These are a few of the things we did:

### Her name is "mom!"

We let them know they were dealing with a person called "mom," not just another prisoner on death row. We insisted that every doctor and every nurse call her by her first name (or "mom") and that she be treated like a person, not a statistic.

## Clear, honest, factual, "no drama" communication

We educated ourselves on her disease and began to alter our dialog with the medical personnel so that our line of questioning became less dramatic and emotional and more precise. We found that once the doctors knew they were interacting with people who could understand them, they were more willing to be specific and exact with the details of our mother's condition. Clear, honest, "no drama" communication is a key factor in developing a stress-free relationship with medical personnel.

## We were "interested" in their lives

I don't care if you're the most modest person in town, everyone likes to talk about themselves and everyone wants to tell their story. I learned a trick a long time ago: If you really want to be interesting to people, all you have to do is be *interested* in them. To the degree you are interested in who they are, what they do, and how they got to be where they are, to that degree they are *interested* in you. Try it; it works. So I started to get interested in the personal life of my mother's doctor.

"Why did he choose medicine?"

"Was being a doctor all it was cracked up to be?"

"What about his family?"

"Does the job interfere with his social life?"

A normal person began to emerge from behind the white coat, a "regular guy" who just happened to be a doctor, an average fellow with family problems, money problems, career problems, and a mother. I would always ask him about his mother. It seemed the more we talked about *his*

**129**

mother, the more interest he took in mine. The point is, in no time at all, the way my mother's doctor communicated with us began to shift from bland, confusing medical narrative, to understandable, caring, honest conversation.

## The power of acknowledgement

We are all suckers for a complement and so are doctors. The more I acknowledged him, the better care he took of my mother, simple as that. I even sent a letter to his superior complementing the degree of care my mother was getting, and the result was my phone calls were returned immediately, if not sooner. The practice of acknowledgment can be a powerful, effective aid in achieving any desired result with another human being.

Now, you might think that I'm suggesting you use these techniques as a sneaky ploy to persuade doctors and nurses to pay closer attention to your parent's needs over the concerns of other patients. THAT'S EXACTLY WHAT I'M TELLING YOU TO DO! We are talking about taking good care of your parent, while still enjoying an anxiety-free life of your own! The more you can persuade professional medical personnel to communicate clearly and directly with you, the easier and less stressful your interaction with them will be.

Your parent's doctor is now an intricate part of the family. All diagnostic and medical services should be approved by him or at least his opinion should be taken into consideration. When necessary, your parent's physician can make important referrals to a specialist, hospital, or other valuable services that you could not obtain without doctor approval. It is important for you to establish a good relationship with your parent's doctor and all the other medical personnel that interact with him.

**The following "tips" are designed to help you interact with medical personnel and remind you of the importance of quality geriatric health care:**

• Clear, "drama-free" communication is crucial to achieving straightforward, honest dialog with medical personnel.
• It is extremely difficult for doctors when they have to explain details to so many family members. One person should be assigned the task of "medical communicator" for the entire family. It does not have to be the oldest or the most mature, however, it should be the person who is most likely to understand and interpret your parent's condition.
• If your parent is hospitalized, don't allow doctors and nurses to speak condescendingly to him, i.e., baby talk, etc. Politely request that they speak straight to your parent like an adult.
• Because our parents are living longer, preventative health care is crucial to increasing the quality of their lives.
• Supporting your parents in achieving and maintaining good health should be your most important objective. As long as they remain healthy, the job of caring for them is less strenuous.
• Good health is a result of mental stimulation and physical activity.
• Type a list of all the medicines your parents take and double-check the spelling. Always have a copy with you, as well as a few copies around the house. Discard all medicines that are outdated or not currently in use.
• Don't give up trying to ease your parent's pain. After the

traditional doctors have given up, try the untraditional. Chinese medicine, chiropractic therapy, acupuncture...as long as they are a licensed, reputable therapist that comes recommended, the chance of doing any harm is nil. Just keep making up ways to end your parent's suffering. It will surely end your emotional strain if you can help lessen your parent's physical pain.

• Always get a second opinion for important medical procedures.

• Be sensitive to your parents' changing health and educate yourself on their medical condition.

• Insist that your parents continue regular physical and dental checkups.

• Interview potential doctors for your parents *before* you hire one. Make sure they are experienced, knowledgeable experts in the field of geriatric medicine.

• Old people often find it difficult to correctly identify their pains or interpret their own physical condition. They get frightened, and the fear itself can lead to severe anxiety attacks or even stroke. When it comes to their health, you must learn to recognize the difference between when they are really sick and when they are simply not feeling well. However, never guess. When in doubt, consult a doctor.

• The commitment is to your parents' safety and painless comfort, not so much longevity. We've figured out how to keep people alive longer, but we have yet to determine how to increase the quality of their life.

• Educate yourself on Medicare, Medicaid, Medigap, and other types of health insurance for your parents (see Chapter 11, Family Business).

# Chapter 19

# HEARING LOSS

*Secondary comments and peripheral noise make up
over 50% of our total conversational understanding.*

Deafness deserves its own chapter because hearing loss is one of the most common disabilities associated with aging. It can also be the most misunderstood. What you might suspect as senility or dementia could be loss of hearing.

My father has severe hearing loss and has managed to conceal it most of his life. He has always been ashamed of it, and until he retired, refused to wear a hearing aid. Consequently, he has mastered the art of saying "uh-huh" in such a way that people think he understands what they said, but he really doesn't. This blatant cover-up has embarrassed him many times. By denying his hearing loss and "faking" most conversations, he has missed out on those "secondary comments" which make up more than half of our conversational dialog. Over the years, as educated as he is, his ability to conduct an intelligent conversation has been sadly limited.

Those with even slight deafness often have a tendency to withdraw from "one-on-one" conversations and stay clear of group situations where common background noise interferes with conversational dialog. When people don't hear fully, they don't understand fully, therefore they often make inaccurate judgments or react in "non sequiturs," which can result in apprehension and stress. This lack of understanding also leads to mood swings, paranoia, depression, and erratic behavior, which could easily be mistaken for senility or dementia.

**If your parent has any of the following symptoms, have his hearing checked immediately. By improving his hearing, you could end those incessant misunderstandings that drive you crazy.**

- Your parent consistently doesn't understand movies, TV shows, jokes, etc.
- He mispronounces names.
- He becomes quiet around people.
- He can't always hear the phone or if someone is at the door.
- He pretends to understand what is being said, but it's obvious he doesn't.
- He accuses you of whispering or not speaking loud enough.
- He constantly asks people to repeat what they have just said.
- He acts more paranoid than usual.
- He always turns up the volume on the TV, radio, VCR, CD player, etc.

**134**

- He complains about all the noise going on in the background.
- Your parent gets easily depressed.


## Recommendations:

• Request that your parents have a hearing checkup with a specialist.
• Educate yourself on the various types of hearing loss.
• Be aware of the similarity between hearing loss and mental illness.

I recommend that you send a contribution to:

Children Of Deaf Adults (CODA)
P.O. Box 30715
Santa barbara, CA 93130
(805) 682-0997

Deafness Research Foundation
9 East 38th Street
New York, NY 10016-003
(212) 684-6556

National Association of the Deaf (NAD)
814 Thayer Ave.
Silver Springs, MD 20910
(301) 587-1788

# Chapter 20

# ALZHEIMER'S, DEMENTIA, AND SENILITY

*"I can remember World War II in complete detail, but I can't remember where I put my keys."*

Alzheimer's disease is a progressive, dementing illness which will touch one-third of all American families. Symptoms include memory loss, impairments in reasoning and judgement, loss of effective communication skills, physical deterioration, disorientation, and often, a change in personality. Alzheimer's is the fourth leading cause of death among older Americans. The risk of developing Alzheimer's before age 50 is less than 1%. Immediate family relatives of Alzheimer's patients have a 50% chance of developing the disease because the tendency is transmitted as an "autosomal dominant trait." At the present time, the cause of the disease is unclear, and there is no known cure and no truly effective therapy.

Research for Alzheimer's has been recently escalated by increased media attention and greater public concern. Hopefully, this new public awareness, along with your contributions, will lead to new medical breakthroughs for combating this devastating disease.

I recommend you send a donation to:
Alzheimer's Disease and Related Disorders Assoc., Inc.
919 North Michigan Ave., Suite 1000
Chicago, IL 60611-1676
(312) 335-8700

## Senility

Senility is a declining condition associated with aging and characterized by mental incompetence and emotional instability. The cause of this condition is said to be the aging process itself; however, current studies have found that social isolation, malnutrition, severe anxiety, apathy, depression, loss of a mate, and other social or emotional factors can all contribute to the senile syndrome. Research has shown that increased social activity, continued family interaction, and psychiatric intervention can help to reverse senile behavior.

## Dementia

Dementia is the irreversible deterioration of mental abilities and intellectual functions. Dementia is not a disease itself—it is the result of various symptoms that accompany certain diseases. There are a variety of diseases and conditions that cause dementia including schizophrenia, Alzheimer's, senility, brain damage caused by injury, Parkinson's disease, Huntington's disease, Pick's disease, and others.

**138**

## Depression

Depression is a psychological condition evidenced by sadness, unusual behavior, difficulty in thinking, inability to concentrate, inactivity, feelings of dread, occasional suicidal thoughts, etc. Unlike dementia, depression can be reversed and treated with satisfactory results.

## "I don't know who my parent is anymore."

I know you're frustrated with the person your parent has become, and I realize that what you would really like to do is shake your parent and tell him to "snap out of it!" But you must begin to accept the fact that your parent is mentally ill. He will say and do crazy things, but he can't help it — he's sick. Think of it this way: If you had an older brother named Jimmy, and he was mentally ill, you might get frustrated once in a while, or occasionally impatient, but you wouldn't allow Jimmy to "get to you" because you know that's just the way he is. Well, your parent is Jimmy! Love your parent, care for him, and make him as happy as possible. BUT DON'T ALLOW THE WAY HE IS TO GET TO YOU! Don't allow your parent's mental sickness to tear at your emotions, and don't take what he says personally. If he walks outside naked, or insists that you are a selfish, no-good kid who is intentionally trying to harm him, realize that this is not coming from the parent you used to know. It's coming from Jimmy, and he is only expressing his mental confusion.

Listen, I know that what I'm suggesting is easier said than done, but you're getting this straight from experience because I am currently caring for a Jimmy — my own father. When I attempt to interact with my dad the way I used to in the past, I get nowhere, because he does not respond to me the way he used to. However, when I care for him the same way I would care for a mentally ill brother, his disparaging actions and comments simply roll off me, because I realize that this is his illness talking, not the father I used to know.

When your parent's ability to function normally has changed, and there is absolutely no hope of reversing it, the manner in which you interact with him must also change. When you can finally shift the way you interact with your mentally ill parent from a child who is hoping that things will turn out, to an adult child who accepts the truth, only then will you be able to give quality, loving care to your parent, without the additional weight of emotional stress.

## Recommendations

• First, determine if your parent is suffering from Alzheimer's, senility, hearing loss, depression, dementia, etc.
• If a form of dementia is diagnosed, act immediately. Call a family meeting and plan now for a future that is going to get more challenging.
• Educate yourself on your parent's particular problem.
• Communicate with the doctor and determine together what care/treatment is required.
• Determine how care will be paid for.
• Divide time and financial responsibilities equally among family and friends.
• Investigate the possibility of a "visiting nurse" that specializes in dementia-related problems.
• Join a support group. You are not alone.

# Chapter 21

# WHEN IT'S "TERMINAL"

*Your willingness to communicate the truth*
*will ultimately free you from the constraints of regret.*

The experience of waiting for your parent to die can produce the most unusual collection of emotions, feelings, and sensations ever assembled at the same time for one event. It seems as though all your emotions wrestle each other to get your attention. One after another, your worst fears tug at your character with weary abandon and your wildest fantasies dance with your thoughts, as if this terrible time in your life was simply some sort of whimsical, eerie dream...actually more like a nightmare.

A phenomenon I call "Multiple Emotional Overload" is truly a bizarre experience. First, there's the **pain** of losing a parent and the **sadness** over his/her impending fate. And even though you've done all you can to ease your parent's pain and assure his comfort, you still experience a sense of **failure**. Then the memories...oh the memories. Every time you look at a family photo or reminisce about a special time, there's no holding back the **sorrow** that overwhelms you, followed by **anger** that this event is happening at this time in your life. Then there's the **apprehension** of "what will life be like without him?" — immediately followed by the **relief** that "It" will all be over soon. **Hope** comes along at its tired, petty pace, and you begin to think that a miracle is a strong possibility. After all, you've read about people miraculously recovering from terrible illnesses all the time. Then your **faith** shows up out of the blue. You blame God, then you remind Him that your parent was really a good person and ask God to watch over him. Then you blame God again. You may even experience **fear** of the unknown, which causes you to ask, "Where exactly is my parent going?" Perhaps followed by **jealously** that he gets to move on to the next world and you must stay behind. Then your mind begins to vote on the exact day and time that it's going to happen — "I really have a feeling that 'It' is going to happen tomorrow" — only to see your parent live through another day, all of this followed by **confusion** as to your role in his dying process, as well as a feeling of **guilt** that you're not doing enough.

Then there are the physical manifestations of this plague of events — nausea, diarrhea, and stomach aches from not eating properly, backaches, body aches, and cramps from sitting or sleeping on hospital furniture, and anxiety and headaches from thinking and worring too much.

And if the emotional and physical strain doesn't get to you, the telephone will. Being on 24-hour call, day after day, night after night, waiting for the phone to ring can be a tense, nerve-racking ordeal. And every time it rings, it shocks your nervous system and sends a jolt directly through your heart. Especially if it rings at an odd hour, then you KNOW this is it! You KNOW that someone on the other end of the phone is about to say the words you've been dreading all your life.

"I'm sorry to inform you that your parent has...."

It's a dramatic, frustrating time in your life and eventually the emotional strain, the physical stress, and the intrusion into your privacy begin to challenge your self-confidence and diminish your strength.

However, there is a small, flickering light at the end of this dark tunnel. You must realize that you have a right to experience every one of your human emotions, anytime you choose, anytime they show up. Do not hold them inside. Give yourself permission to experience all of your emotions as they arise. If you're sitting at the side of your terminally ill parent and a sudden feeling of happiness and joy overwhelms you, don't deny it, don't try to figure it out, and don't stuff the emotion simply because you think it's inappropriate. Experience it — privately perhaps — but experience it. Who knows why it showed up, and who cares! Maybe you have a thought that you want your parent to hurry up and die and get it over with. Go ahead and have the thought, then go ahead and feel guilty about it if that's what follows. These feelings are yours to experience, and they are absolutely not to be shut out, withheld, or denied. If you keep them in, they will eventually manifest themselves out in other ways. The most common consequence of withheld expression is physical illness and mental anxiety. One way to manage the madness is to notice that your feelings don't have much to do with the outcome of the situation, your emotions cannot judge the events of the future, and your crazy thoughts have nothing to do with whether or not your parent lives or dies. So give yourself permission to be nuts for a while. Go ahead and fully experience your feelings and let go with your emotions. Just don't get hooked by them or take any action or make any decisions based on them. If grief shows up, go ahead and grieve, then let it go. If anger shows up, go ahead and be angry, then allow it to pass. Your feelings are going to come up no matter what you do so you might as well experience them, then let them go.

To the degree that you can simply have your emotions when they arise — to really own them, to experience them and express them — to that degree they will pass quickly. By experiencing and expressing your feelings and emotions, you are inherently giving yourself permission to live life to its fullest, thereby confirming your emotional stability and sustaining your precious vitality.


## Their final conversation

My mother suffered from heart disease and complications of the lungs for many years. However, it ultimately took her three months to die. Almost every night of that three months — and I'm not exaggerating — nearly every night, a doctor would say, "We don't think she's going to make it through the night." My sister and I made a deal that we would not let her die alone. We took turns spending the night at the hospital. It became a ritual, a vigil. It was like I was working a double shift.

One night it was my turn to stay at the hospital. It was about 12:30 a.m. I was sitting next to mom's bed, and we were watching TV. I noticed she was sort of daydreaming and crying a little — it was obvious she was struggling with something. I repeatedly asked what was wrong, and she answered as often, "Oh...nothing." Finally I said, "Mom, I know you...there is something bothering you...what is it?" Reluctantly she said, "Well, Mike...I want to be buried in my gold dress." "Oh boy," I thought. This is the conversation I've been waiting for. My heart started to pound. I figured if she was tough enough to talk about it, then I was tough enough to listen.

"Okay mom, " I said. "What else?"

"All the insurance papers are in the top drawer of my bedroom bureau, " she said.

"Yes...go on, mom. " I grabbed a pen and paper and began to write.

"Your father can't take care of himself. Be sure to find a good 'live-in' person to help."

"Okay, got it...what else?"

We went on and on talking about a variety of important issues, literally preparing for a future that she would have no part in. After we had gone over all the household issues, I began to ask her questions about the family.

"What do you think about Uncle Joe, mom?"

"He's a good brother to me...I don't get to see him as often as I would like but I love him," she said, teary-eyed.

"What about Ray across the street?"

"He's my best friend," she said. "You be sure and look in on him from time to time."

That night I asked her about every friend and relative she had, and she had a comment for all of them — not always a good comment, but this was her chance to make a final statement about everyone in her life — to finally be complete with the people in her life so she could move on, uninhibited by withheld thoughts or communications.

(By the way, even though my sister and I were committed to not allowing our mother to die alone, she finally did die alone, on the one and only evening we left her by herself.)

The thing about the dying process is that everybody

**145**

knows it's going to happen, everybody wants to talk about it, and nobody has the courage (or the words) to say anything. There may be a time when your dying parent wants to talk about future family affairs or funeral arrangements, and you may have a tendency to avoid the conversation. The most difficult thing is to talk to your dying parent about a tomorrow they will never know. But this is a time to be strong. Your dying parent needs to re-examine his/her past, feel complete that important family matters are taken care of, and have a sense that all will be well in the future. Too many times people die without saying what it is they need to say in order to be complete with this world before going on to the next. Do not deny them, or yourself, this opportunity. It can be as valuable to you as it is to them.

### Your final conversation

You always hear stories about the guilt that adult children carry around after their parents die:
"I should have told them I loved them."
"I should have thanked them."
"I wanted to tell them before they died but I just couldn't."
If you avoid the opportunity to fully express what you want to say to your parent before he/she dies, you run the risk of carrying around useless regret for the rest of your life.
I can remember when I was 11-years-old, my mother took me to a sporting goods store to buy a baseball glove. The one I wanted was much more expensive than the one we could afford. I watched as my mom switched price tags. She whispered to me, "Don't say anything." Now I knew this was wrong, but heck, I got the glove, and it was my mother

doing the bad thing, not me. An innocent incident? Maybe. But I carried the thought that my mother was a dishonest person all the way to adulthood.

A week before she died, I reminded her of the incident and told her that I held the secret all these years. Now, the truth is, my mom was a very honest person. At first, she did not remember the incident, then she began to laugh a bit and explained to me that she always wanted me to have the best things, and she was sorry that the incident had affected me so much. When I left the hospital that night, I felt great; I know it seems silly, but it was a big one for me. To my mother, it was nothing, but to me, it meant I wouldn't have to carry that one around after she was gone.

Now is the time to take a look and see if there is anything you need to say to your dying parent that will complete it for you. Maybe you're already complete, and you honestly don't need to say anything. But I encourage you to look deep. Look into your heart and see if there is anything you are holding back. It may be something you think has no meaning or is silly to bring up at this time — perhaps an old upset or a misunderstanding that you would like to clear up with them. You may think that your past peeves are petty in comparison to what they're going through, and you're probably right. But left unexpressed, those withheld communications can develop into chronic regret — feelings that could take months of personal therapy to clean up. Now you have an opportunity to avoid that scenario and be complete with your parent before he/she dies. If he is unconscious, or in a coma, you can write him a letter and read it to him. Your parent may not be able to respond to you, but chances are he can hear you. And even if he can't, it's your willingness to communicate the truth that will ultimately free you from the constraints of regret.

## Hospice

People who work in hospices should be awarded the medal of honor. "Hospice" is a philosophy of care for people who are terminally ill. The purpose of a hospice is to provide comfort and support, rather than a cure. A hospice creates an atmosphere in which the patient can complete life with dignity, independence, and peace. A hospice also provides emotional support to the surviving family during time of bereavement.

## Facts about hospice:

- Hospice care is covered under Medicare and other insurance plans that include home health care benefits and hospital care. Private donations are also accepted.
- Hospice service is a team effort including the patient, doctor, family, friends, and hospice staff.
- Hospice care is available to patients who are no longer under treatment for cure of their disease and whose life expectancy is six months or less.
- The patient and the family must understand that the care given in a hospice is for comfort, not cure.
- Each hospice provides its own special services, which can include skilled home care, consultation services, spiritual counseling, special nursing needs, etc.
- Depending on the community in which you live, hospice care may be limited to a private home, or may include an outpatient facility.
- The hospice will administer prescribed drugs such as morphine to aid the patient's comfort, rather than prolong his/her life.

## Euthanasia

Active or passive euthanasia is the act of inducing a gentle, painless death. In the United States, active euthanasia is unlawful. In some countries, active euthanasia, or "mercy killing," is treated as a special crime with lighter penalties.

Passive euthanasia is roughly defined as the practice of not prolonging the life of a suffering person whose disease is inevitably fatal. It is considered by many physicians to be a good medical practice. But the decision not to artificially prolong life must be granted by the mentally alert patient, or through a previously executed "living will." In 1990, the U.S. Supreme Court ruled that people who make their wishes known have a constitutional right to have life-sustaining treatment discontinued. In the cases of permanently unconscious persons who have left no clear instructions, the state may deny the request of family members to terminate treatment. This ruling gave legal backing to the "living will," which provides evidence of a person's desire not to be kept alive by artificial means should that person become terminally ill or incompetent (see Chapter 11, Family Business).

## Morphine

When someone is terminally ill, suffering, or in pain, the doctor or hospital may prescribe morphine to ease the pain and comfort the patient. Morphine is an organic compound extracted from opium and used as a light anesthetic, or as a sedative.

When my mother was in her last days, she was in extreme

**149**

pain from angina and suffering from a lack of oxygen. Even though she received a constant flow of oxygen, she still had a hard time breathing. One day I was holding her in my arms and she was gasping for air and begging me to help her. The one and only savior was morphine. Whenever she took her dose of the drug, it would relax her and ease her anxiety so she could sleep and breathe easier. Toward the end, it seemed we were asking the doctor to give her additional morphine injections every couple of hours. She would wake only to suffer pain and anxiety till the next injection, then she would sleep.

Finally, the doctor said he could prescribe a "morphine drip," which meant she would probably rest comfortably but never regain consciousness. I wasn't available for this discussion, so my sister was on her own with this decision. It was a tough one, because it meant we would probably never talk to our mother again. Reluctantly, my sister made the decision to go for the "drip," and it turned out to be the best. My mom died in her sleep 24 hours later completely painless and free of anxiety.

When there is absolutely no hope of recovery whatsoever, and when your parent is suffering, "passive euthanasia" seems to be the closest to a peaceful passing with dignity.

### The dying process

There are a variety of signs that signal when the person has entered into the final phase of the dying process.
**Withdrawal**: Your parent may seem distant and unresponsive. This indicates preparation for release and a detaching of physical surroundings and personal relationships. Hear-

ing often remains all the way to the end, so it would be best to talk to your parent in your normal tone of voice, identify yourself by name, hold his/her hand, and say whatever you need to say that will help your parent "let go."

**Disorientation**: Your parent may seem confused about the time, place, and even who you are. Identify yourself when you speak and tell your parent truthfully where he is and why he is there.

**Restlessness**: Your parent may make restless and repetitive motions with his arms and body. This is normal, due in part to pain-relieving drugs, metabolic changes, and a decrease in circulation to the brain. Do not attempt to restrain such motions. Lightly massage your parent's forehead or his hands and speak in a natural, quiet way. Reading or soft music may soothe your parent's anxiety.

**Change in appetite**: Your parent may begin to refuse food. Do not force him to eat. Give him only what he requires for his comfort.

**Change in breathing:** There is a symptom called "Cheyne-Stokes Syndrome." It indicates a decrease in circulation to the vital internal organs. This is a common occurrence. Elevating your parent's head and softly massaging his hands and forehead may bring comfort.

**Social isolation:** Your parent may indicate that he only wants to be with certain people, most likely the persons he needs support from the most. If you are not invited into this select group, don't be offended. It only means your parent has completed with you, and it's now time to say good-bye. If you are among this group, it means that he still needs your support and permission to let go.

**Unusual comments:** Your parent may say things that are completely out of character. A friend of mine's dying father kept repeating, "Your father died of complications due to old age." This is a normal reaction to what your parent is going through emotionally. Don't get hooked by these comments or take offense, rather agree with your parent and comfort him as best as you can.

**Visions and hallucinations:** Your parent may insist that he has seen or spoken to persons that have already died, or has been to a place he calls heaven. These events may be very real to him. Do not try to explain away these claims, rather support your parent, as well as assure him that these are normal occurrences.

## Recommendations

• Go ahead and have the conversations with your parent that you've been avoiding.

• If your parent is dying, or death is imminent, investigate "hospices" in your community. They provide a variety of services for dying people, including setting it up so that your parent can die at home.

• If you are going to discuss your parent's condition or death, either talk about it out loud or leave the room. Your parent may not be alert, but chances are he can hear every word you are saying.

• This unusual and unreasonable parade of feelings and emotions is very common during emotionally demanding times.

• Don't deny your parent (or yourself) the opportunity to talk about his fate. It can be as valuable to him as it is to you.

• Tell the truth about death. The dying person knows it anyway.

• Make funeral arrangements ahead of time (see Chapter

11 Family Business).
• Elderly people usually accept death more willingly than the young.
• Read the book *On Death And Dying* by Elisabeth Kubler-Ross.

My thanks to the Nathan Adelson Hospice in Las Vegas, Nevada, for providing many of the facts contained in this chapter (see Appendix).

Chapter 22

# DEATH

*The loss of a parent is an unparalleled primal loss.*

Nothing compares to the loss of a parent. You might experience terrible things in your life, but nothing touches you quite as profoundly. Some suggest that the loss of a mate is the most traumatic, but the loss of a parent is an unparalleled primal loss. Anyone who has experienced the death of a parent knows there is something profound and final about it.

At the turn of the century, most Americans died in their homes before they turned 50-years-old. Death was regarded as a familiar and expected event and was treated as a public ritual where family, friends, and community members gathered at the home of the deceased to pay their last respects, often around the death bed. Today, the ritual has become a bit more private. However, friends and family are still eager to show their respects and express their grief.

**The following recommendations and suggestions are designed to help you deal with the various circumstances surrounding the death of your parent:**

• When friends and relatives say, "I always loved your parent...is there anything I can do?" take them up on the offer. Don't attempt to make all the arrangements yourself. Give away some of the responsibilities so that you can be with closer family members.
• If the death occurs at home and you did not make prior arrangements with a funeral home, call the doctor, the morturary, or the coroner. They will advise you of what to do next.
• If there is to be a religious service, contact your parent's clergy.
• Don't deprive your friends and relatives of the opportunity to express their feelings with cards and flowers. They want to say good-bye, too, and they want you to know that they have compassion for what you're going through.

**Within the first two weeks of your parent's death:**

• Shift the focus to the surviving parent, or to your own family members.
• Disperse personal belongings as soon as possible.
• Contact the attorney who will be handling the estate.
• Cancel all credit cards.
• Notify the insurance company of any claims.
• Transfer all bank accounts.

## Getting complete after they die

If you did not have the opportunity to say all the things to your parent that you wanted to say, it's not too late. Honest communication is the path to completion. Either sit down with a friend or relative and say exactly what you would tell your parent if he were still alive, or write your parent a letter and stick it in the mail box — let the post office deal with its destination. The important thing is to liberate your withheld communications honestly, so you can get on with your life, free of regret. Your parent does not have to be present for you to fully experience a sense of completion with him.

## How long does the grieving process last?

I am personally in favor of grieving as little as possible in this lifetime. However, there is a common thinking that says the mourning process last approximately one year. The reason is simple: It takes a year to get through all the "firsts" — the first Christmas without your loved one, the first birthday, the first anniversary, etc. Although this is certainly not a hard, fast rule — and again, I cast my vote for short-time grieving — a year seems to be the generally accepted mourning period in our society. Keep in mind that each personal circumstance is special. If you have spent the last year at your parent's bedside expecting and preparing for his death, you may actually experience a sense of completion when it's finally over and not grieve quite as long as a person whose parent died abruptly without warning.

It goes without saying that each situation is unique and the length of time a person spends grieving is an individual decision.

# EPILOGUE

In Chapter Two, I reminded you that your life comes first — your life must take precedence if you are expected to provide good care for your parents and still enjoy your own autonomy. The notion that "your life comes first" is actually a human right. You have the inalienable right to prioritize your life in such a way that you come first. However, there is a danger of misusing that freedom by confusing it with selfish intentions, particularly with regard to your aging parents. For example, they may ask you to do something that is inconvenient, and you just don't want to do it or you just don't feel like doing it, and you may choose to hide behind the notion that "your life comes first," therefore they'll just have to wait.

About a month after my mother died, my 80-year-old father called me one night around 11:45. At first, I thought he just wanted small talk, but the longer we talked, the more I noticed he was avoiding something. Every time I said, "Well, dad, I have to get up early," he would change the subject and keep talking. Finally, he asked me something that seemed extremely difficult for him. He asked me in such a way that he was sure I would say no. His question was, "Would you like to...uh...I don't suppose you would like to...uh...go out for a hot fudge sundae...would ya?" Before I could answer he said, "Oh, never mind...I should probably go to bed anyway...it's late" — immediately followed by, "You know... your mother and I used to go out for a hot fudge sundae about this time of night, oh...once a week or so."

TALK ABOUT HITTING BELOW THE BELT! I live about 25 minutes from his house, it was midnight, and I had to get up early. I absolutely did not want to go. "No way," I thought. "I have to work tomorrow! Why me? This is my life! I don't want to get out of bed and drive all the way to his house, then go out looking for an open restaurant that sells hot fudge sundaes, then sit there and listen to the stories of his past that I've heard a million times, while he drips hot fudge on his pajama top! NO...DAMN IT! NOT TONIGHT...PLEASE, MAKE IT GO AWAY!!"

When I finally got home at 2 a.m., I knew I had done the right thing. Perhaps I felt sorry for him, or maybe it was that child-like quality in his voice that reminded me of when I was a kid and he would take me to get ice cream. But the reward of going out of my way — doing something I did not want to do, validated for me the fact that what "my life comes first" really means is, I have a choice. I have the right to choose whether or not to do something that could be uncomfortable. But it's the freedom to choose that takes precedence over the pain of the choice.

It's true, your life does come first, and no one can take that right from you. But don't use that line as a ploy to escape the responsibility of taking good care of your parents. A sure way out of the madness of parent care is to simply look at what's wanted and needed, then provide it. That's the most honest action you can take, and being honest with yourself is the key to the stress-free care of your parent.

Even though I was aware that "my life comes first," I quickly recognized that what was wanted and needed was ice cream for my dad. I could have chosen not to go, but if I had, I would have missed out on a precious experience with my father and a fabulous hot fudge sundae!

# HONORABLE MENTION

An organization called Children Of Aging Parents (CAPS) deserves honorable mention because they are committed to helping you deal with the stress and problems that can accompany the care of your aging parents.

Since 1977, CAPS has been dedicated to the needs of the caregivers of elderly parents, spouses, relatives, and friends and has become a leader in providing invaluable resources and information to caregivers across the country.

**A few of the services offered by CAPS:**

• Programs, workshops, and seminars for caregivers and professionals.
• In-service training programs to hospital staff, long-term care facility staff, home care agencies, and other professionals.
• Educational presentations to schools, service organizations, senior centers, and religious organizations.

## CAPS MEMBERSHIP ENTITLES YOU TO:

**The CAPSule:** A bi-monthly newsletter that addresses the practical concerns of caregivers, including financial information, emotional issues, national resources, local support groups, etc.

**Networking:** CAPS publishes a national directory called "Care Sharing" which lists hundereds of organizations around the country that provide support and information to the care giver.

**Telephone consultation:** A well-trained, dedicated staff responds and listens to your needs in a sympathetic and empathetic manner and offers information and emotional support.

**Caregiver Support Groups:** a nationwide network of caregiver support groups that can meet your immediate needs and concerns.

**Related literature:** CAPS also maintains a varied selection of resource materials, which includes journals, newsletters, and pamphlets on every subject from Long Distance Caregiving to Caring for the Caregiver. An extensive bibliography related to caregiving is maintained and a list of catalogs of products for the elderly is offered.

I urge you to become a member of CAPS. Call or write to them today:
Children Of Aging Parents (CAPS)
Woodbourne Office Campus, Suite 302-A
1609 Woodbourne Road
Levittown, PA 19057
(215) 945-6900

**164**

# APPENDIX

Many of the following organizations offer informational brochures and pamphlets, memberships, support groups, advice, counseling, etc. These organizations contribute unmatched support for you and your parents. I recommend that you support them with a donation. Also, due to the transient nature of non-profit organizations, some of the following numbers and addresses are subject to change.

**Gray Panthers**
1424 16th St. NW
Washington, DC 20036
(202) 387-3111

**Department of Aging**
1600 K Street
Sacramento, CA 95814
(916) 322-5290

**L.A. City Department of Aging**
600 South Spring St. #900
Los Angeles, CA 90014
(213) 485-4402

**National Council on Aging**
600 Maryland Ave. S.W. West Wing 100
Washington, DC 20024
(202) 479-1200

**Alzheimer's Disease &**
**Related Disorders Assoc. Inc.**
919 N. Michigan, Suite 1000
Chicago, IL 60611-1676
(800) 272-3900

**The Nathan Adelson Hospice**
4141 S. Swenson Ave.
Las Vegas, NE 89119
(702) 733-0320

**American Association**
**of Retired Persons (AARP)**
800 523-5800
1909 "K" Street
Washington, DC 20049

**American Society on Aging**
833 Market Street, Suite 512
San Francisco, CA 94103-1824
(415) 882-2910

**U.S. Department of**
**Health And Human Services**
**Office of Human**
**Development Services,**
**Administration On Aging**
Washington, DC 20024
(202) 619-0257

**Senior Service Team**
1250 Morena Blvd.
San Diego, CA 92110
(619) 692-8787

**Adult Children of**
**Aging Parents**
**St. Joseph Hospital**
**Community Outreach**
1100 West Stewart Dr.
Orange, CA 92668
(714) 771-8243

**Community Outreach &**
**Counseling Service**
P.O. Box 5600
Orange, CA 92613-5600
(714) 771-8243

**Support Group For**
**Children Of Seniors**
**Palo Alto Senior Center**
450 Bryant St.
Palo Alto, CA 94301
(415) 327-2811

**Adult Children of**
**Aging Parents**
**Jewish Family Services**
1600 Scott St.
San Francisco, CA 94115
(415) 567-8861

166

You And Your Aging Relatives
Catholic Charities
1049 Market St. #200
San Francisco, CA 94103
(415) 864-7400

Children Of Aging Parents
123 W. Gutierrez St.
Santa Barbara, CA 93101

Goleta Valley Hospital.
Ashton Center
5333 Hollister Ave.
Santa Barbara, CA 93111
(805) 965-1001

Western Division
Mental Health Assn.
8912 Volunteer Lane, # 210
Sacramento, CA 95826
(916) 368-3100

California Self-Help Center
U.C.L.A. Psychology Dept.
405 Hilgard Ave.
Los Angeles, CA 90024
(213) 825-1799

Grown-ups With
Aging Parents
5555 N. Fresno St.
Fresno, CA 93710
(209) 439-4770

Well Spouse Foundation
Support Groups
P.O. Box 28876
San Diego, CA 92128

Children of Aging Parents
(CAPS)
National Headquarters
Woodbourne Office Campus
1609 Woodbourne Road
Levittown, PA 19057
(215) 945-6900

Caregiver Support Group
Olmsted Co. Health
Department
1650 Fourth St., SE
Rochester, MN 55904
(507) 285-8349

Caregiver Support Group
Catholic Charities
207 Seventh Ave., N.
St. Cloud, MN 56301
(612) 252-1848

**United District Hospital**
**Laugh a Lots Support Group**
401 Prairie Ave., N.
Staples, MN 56479
(218) 894-1515

**Caregivers**
**Sunrise District Center**
2399 Cedar Ave.
White Bear Lake, MN 55110
(612) 429-0543

**We're Not Alone**
204 Alida Street
Clarksdale, MS 38614
(601) 624-2819

**Support Group Clearinghouse**
**Kansas City Assn. for Mental**
**Health**
706 West 42nd St.
Kansas City, MO 64111
(816) 561-HELP

**Caregivers of Older Persons**
**Candlelight Care Center**
1201 Hunt Ave.
Columbia, MO 65202
(314) 875-3494, (314) 449-1448

**Supportworks**
1012 Kings Drive, Suite 923
Charlotte, NC 28283
(704) 331-9500

**Caregiver Support Group**
**Gaston County Dept. of Aging/**
**Adult Day Care**
901 South New Hope Road
Gastonia, NC 28054
(704) 866-3800

**Caring for Aging Parents**
**Wesley Long Community**
**Hospital**
501 North Elam Ave, PO
Drawer X3
Greensboro, NC 27425
(919) 854-6364

**Union County Caregiver**
**Support Group**
**Council on Aging**
PO Box I85
Monroe, NC 28110
(704) 289-1797

**You & Your Aging Parents**
**Council on Aging of Wake**
**County**
401 East Whitaker Mill Road
Raleigh, NC 27608
(919) 755-6444

Our Elders, Our Selves
Senior Services
Tobacco Square
Winston-Salem, NC 27101
(919) 725-0907

Aging Family Support Group
Midland Area Agency on
Aging
PO Box 905, 305 N. Hastings
Hastings, NE 68902
(402) 463-4565

Living Room
Support Group for Families
with Aging Relatives
900 N. 90th St.
Omaha, NE 68114
(402) 559-4427

Children of Aging Parents
West Central Services
PO Box 468, Horizon House
Lebanon, NH 03466
(603) 448-5610

Caregivers of Aging Persons
Souhegan Nursing Association
North River Road
Milford, NH 03055
(603) 673-3460

New Jersey Self Help
Clearinghouse
St. Clares Riverside Medical
Center
Pocono Road
Denville, NJ 07834
(800) 367-6274 (201) 625-9565

Sandwich Generation
Northern Valley Older Adult
Day Care
2 Park Avenue
Dumont, NJ 07628
(201) 385-4400

Children of Aging Parents
(CAPS)
Franklin Convalescent Center
Community Room
3371 Route 27
Franklin Park, NJ 08823
(201) 821-8000

Relatives of Aging Persons
(RAP)
Monmouth County Office on
Aging
Hall of Records Annex
Main St.
Freehold Twp., NJ 07728
(201) 431-2920

**169**

Assisting Adult Children of the
Elderly
Camden County Office on
Aging
120 White Horse Pike, Suite 103
Haddon Heights, NJ 08035
(609) 546-6404

Caregivers of the Elderly
Pleasant Valley Adult Day
Care
40 Main Street
Holmdel, NJ 07733
(201) 946-7070

Association of Elderly
Caregivers
Grand & 203 East Wilson Aves.
Moorestown, NJ 08057
(609) 235-0125

HELP Support Group
Adult Day Care Center
Community Services Bldg.
327 Ridgewood Ave
Paramus, NJ 07652
(201) 599-6177

Friends & Relations of Elderly
(FARE)
Somerset County Office on
Aging
P.O. Box 3000
North Bridge & High Sts.
Somerville, NJ 08876
(201) 231-7175

Support Group for Caregivers
of the Elderly
Kennedy Memorial Hospital
Gerontology Center
30 East Laurel Road
Stratford, NJ 08084
(609) 346-7777

Caregivers of the Elderly
Bergen County Social Services
1 Forest Ave.
Teaneck, NJ 07666
(201) 393-4533

Children of Aging Parents
Union Congregational Church
176 Cooper Ave.
Upper Montclair, NJ 07043
(201) 744-7424

Relatives of Aging Persons
(RAP)
Older Adult Services
1810 Macopin Road
West Miltord, NJ 07480
(201) 728-28627

Parenting Our Parents
Professional Nurse Counselors
1330 San Pedro, NE, #107
Albuquerque, NM 87110
(505) 266-6060

Families With Aging Parents
2850 Juliann Way
Reno, NV 89509
(702) 731-9058

Families of Aging Parents
2055 Regent St.
Reno, NV 89509
(702) 323-2575

NY State Self-Help-
Clearinghouse
Richardson Hall
135 Western Ave
Albany, NY 12222
(518) 442-5337

New York City Self-Help
Clearinghouse
PO Box 022812
Brooklyn, NY 11202
(718) 596-6000

National Self-Help
Clearinghouse
Graduate School & Univ.
Center CUNY
25 West 43rd Street, Room 620
New York, NY 10036
(212) 642-2944

Adult Children with Aging
Parents
Amsterdam Memorial
Hospital
Route 30 N.
Amsterdam, NY 12010
(518) 842-3100

Caring for the Caregiver
Southside Hospital Home Care
Dept.
Montauk Highway
Bay Shore, NY 11706
(516) 968-3876

Caregivers of the Elderly
Children of Aged Parents
Lourdes Hospital
169 Riverside Drive
Binghamton, NY 13905
(607) 798-5111 (607) 798-5690

Caregivers Helpline
Mercycare
68 Elm St.
Hornell, NY 14843
(607) 324-6159

Caring For Our Aging Parents
Family Service of Suffolk
County
646 New York Ave.
Huntington, NY 11743
(516) 427-1768

Caregiver.s Support Group
Ulster County Office for the
Aging
PO Box 1800 - 1 Albany Ave.
Kingston, NY 12401
(914) 331-930

You & Your Aging Parents
Jewish Assn. Services for the
Aged
158 Third St.
Mineola, NY 11501
(516) 742-2050

C.A.R.E.
Volunteer Counseling Service
Rockland County
151 South Main St.
New City, NY 10956
(914) 634-5729

Caregiver's Exchange
Discussion Group
St. Margaret's House Library
49 Fulton Street
New York, NY 10038
(212) 766-8122

Caregivers to the Elderly
105 East 22nd St.
4th Floor, Conference Rm. C
New York, NY 10021
(212) 288-1831

Children of Aging Parents
& Other Caregivers
St. Rose of Lima
Catholic Church
Main St.
North Syracuse, NY 13212
(315) 458-0283 (315) 458-2327

Caring for Caregivers
Regional Council on Aging
79 North Clinton Ave.
Rochester, NY 14604
(716) 454-3224

172

Caregiver Support Group
Staten Island Interagency
Council on Aging
88 New Dorp Plaza, Room 105
Staten Island, NY 10306
(718) 981-6226

Senior Day Care Family
Support Group
36 Church Street
Syosset, NY 11791
(516) 921-2730

Catholic Charities
Elderly Support Services
1654 West Irondale St.
Syracuse, NY 13204
(315) 424-1810

Caregiver Support Group
Rensselaer County Dept. for
Aging
1600 Seventh Ave.
Troy, NY 12180
(518) 270-2730

Caregiver Support Group
Menorah Park Adult Day
Health Center
27100 Cedar Road
Cleveland, OH 44122
(216) 831 -6500

Northwest Caregivers Support
Group
Northwest Counselling
Services
1945 Ridgeview Road, Bldg. 3
Columbus, OH 43221
(614) 488-4544

Natural Supports Program
Tulsa Area Agency on Aging
200 Civic Center, Room 1022
Tulsa, OK 74103
(918) 596-7688

The Sandwiched Generation
Phoebe-Devitt
Development Office,
1922 Turner Street
Allentown, PA
(215) 865-6565

The Sandwiched Generation
Christ Church U.C.C. (Memory
Room)
Center & Market Sts.
Bethlehem, PA 18018
(215) 865-6565

ACAPS
Main Line Adult Day Center
119 Radnor Street
Bryn Mawr, PA 19010
(215) 527-4220

**Parenting Parents Support Group**
Trinity Lutheran Church
26 Commerce Street
Chambersburg, PA 17201
(717) 263-8156

**Children of Aging Parents-Central Bucks (CAPS)**
Doylestown Hospital,
Conference Room A
595 West State St.
Doylestown, PA 18901
(215) 794-3278

**Children of Aging Parents (CAPS)**
Rolling Hill Hospital, Main
Bldg, 4th floor
60 E. Township Line Road
Elkins Park, PA 19117
(215) 663-6324

**Caregiver Support Group Aging Services, Inc.**
201 Airport Professional Cr.
Indiana, PA 15701
(412) 349-4500

**Caregiver Support Group North Penn Adult Day Care Center Visiting Nurses**
51 Medical Campus Drive
Lansdale, PA 19446
(215) 855-1298

**Concerned Caregivers Lawrence County Area Agency on Aging**
15 W. Washington St, Suite 201
New Castle, PA 16101-3907
(412) 658-5661

**Children of Aging Parents (CAPS)**
Chandler Hall
Adult Day Center
Buck Road & Barclay Street
Newtown, PA 18940
(215) 945-6900

**Children of Aging Parents (CAPS)**
White Horse Village
Gradyville Road
Newtown Square, PA 19073
(215) 558-5044

**174**

Children of Aging Parents
(CAPS)
Leader I & II Nursing &
Rehab. Center
2004 Old Rich Road
Norristown, PA 19401
(215) 277-0380

Children of Aging Parents
(CAPS)
Chestnut Hill Residence
495 East Abington Avenue
Philadelphia, PA 19118
(215) 247-5307

Children of Aging Parents
(CAPS)
St. Agnes Adult Day Care Center
1900 South Broad St.
Philadelphia, PA 19145
(215) 339-4510

Caregiver Support Group
Philadelphia Center for Older
People
509 S. Broad St.
Philadelphia, PA 19147
(215) 546-5879

Family Support Group
New Opportunities for the
Aging
955 Rivermont Ave.
Pittsburgh, PA 15207
(412) 422-6066

Caregiver Support Groups
Berks County Office of Aging
15 South Eighth Street
Reading, PA 19602-1105
(215) 378-8808

Children of Aging Parents
(CAPS)
Northampton Manor
65 Richboro-Newtown Road (Rt.
332)
Richboro, PA 18954
(215) 945-6900

Family Caregiver Support
Program Group
Office of Human Services
Area Agency on Aging
PO Box A
Ridgway, PA 15853
(814) 776-2200

Caregiver Support Group
Area Agency on Aging
701 Main St.
Towanda, PA 18848

Support Group Helpline
Rhode Island Dept. of Health
Cannon Bldg., Davis St.
Providence, Rl 02908
(401) 277-2231

Alzheimer's Association
Upstate SC Chapter
200 McGee Road
Anderson, SC 29625
(803) 224-3045

Caretakers of the Elderly
Easter Seal Society
8 Aberdeen Drive
Greenville, SC 29605
(803) 242-7195

Coordinated Adult Care
Council
McCormick County Council
on Aging
PO Box 684
McCormick, SC 29835
(803) 465-2626

Winnsboro Family Support
Group
Fairfield County Council on
Aging
210 E. Washington St.
Winnsboro, SC 29180
(803) 635-3015

Adult Children of Aging
Parents
First Lutheran Church
327 South Dakota Ave.
Sioux Falls, SD 57102
(605) 336-3734

Caring for the Elderly:
A Family Support Group
Westside Hospital
Women's Center
Nashville, TN 37203
(615) 356-9411

Caregivers Support Group
Office on Aging
1000 S. Broadway
Carrollton, TX 75006-7214
(214) 242-4464

Alzheimer's Support Group
1502 Airline
Town Plaza Mall Meeting Room
Victoria, TX 77901
(512) 578-1587

**176**

Heart of Texas Family Support
Group
Heart of Texas Elder Services
105 Meadowbrook Drive
Waco, TX 76706

Quality Aging
(Caring for Aging Loved One)
Salt Lake County Aging
Services
2001 South State, Suite S-1500
Salt Lake City, UT 84190-2300
(801) 468-2764

Adult Children Dealing With
Aging Relatives
Woodburn Mental Health Cr.
3340 Woodburn Road
Annandale, VA 22003
(703) 573-0523

Home for Supper
Caregivers Mutual Support
Group
142 Merchants Row
Rutland, VT 05701
(802) 775-3223

Alzheimer's Support Group
Good Samaritan Hospital
Campus
Alzheimer's Resource Center
14th Ave., SE
Puyallup, WA 98372
(206) 845-9748  (206) 848-6661

Caregiver Support Group
Hampshire County Committee
on Aging
PO Box 41
School St. & Birch Ln.
Romney, WV 26757
(304) 822-4097

Caregivers Support Group
Upper Ohio Valley
North Panhandle Area Agency
on Aging
PO Box 2086
Wheeling, WV 26003
(304) 242-1800

Self-Help Clearinghouse of
Metro. Toronto
40 Orchard View Blvd.
Suite 215
Toronto, Ontario M4R 1B9
(416) 487-4355

Care for the Caregivers Project
Mount Saint Vincent
University
166 Bedford Highway
Halifax, Nova Scotia B3M 2J6
(902) 443-4450 x 467

Care for the Caregiver
Jewish Support Services for
the Elderly
5151 Cote Ste. Catherine Road
Montreal, Quebec H3W 1M6
(514) 343-3795

Rainy Day People
Clearinghouse of Self Help
Support Groups
PO Box 472
Scottsdale, AZ 85252
(602) 840-1029

Friends in Deed
Caregivers Support Group
7 South Abrego
Green Valley, AZ 85614
(602) 625-1150

COPE - Caring for Older Persons
Samaritan Health Services
9326 East McDowell Road,
Suite 32
Phoenix, AZ 85006
(602) 239-5844

Caregiver Support Group
Division of Aging (UAMS)
4301 W. Marleham, Slot #622
Little Rock, AR 72201
(501) 661-5282

Southern Tri-City Regional
Self-Help Center
5839 Green Valley Circle,
Suite 100
Culver City, CA 90230
(213) 645-9890

Children of Aging Parents
San Ramon Valley United
Methodist Church
902 Danville Blvd.
Alamo, CA 94507
(415) 837-5243

Caregivers Support Group
Bellflower Health Dept.
10005 E. Flower St.
Bellflower, CA 90706
(714) 521-1178

Coping With Caregiving
Del Oro Regional Resource
Center
3625 Mission Ave. #300
Carmichael, CA 95608
(916) 971-00893

**178**

**Eden Hospital Geriatric Services**
20103 Lake Cabot Road
Castro Valley, CA 94546
(415) 727-2719

**Grown-ups With Aging Parents**
5555 N. Fresno St.
Fresno, CA 93710
(209) 439-4770

**Tides of Time**
PO Box 686
Ft. Bragg, CA 95437
(707) 964-0443

**Caring Children of Aging Parents**
**St. Jude Medical Center**
101 E. Valencia Mesa Dr.
Fullerton, CA 92635
(714) 871-3280 x 3323

**Someone To Turn To**
229 New York Ranch Road
Jackson, CA 95642
(209) 223-0442

**Caring Children of Aging Parents**
6335 Myrtle Ave.
Long Beach, CA 90805
(213) 423-7924

**Caring Children of Aging Parents**
**Los Alamitos Medical Center**
3751 Katella Ave.
Los Alamitos, CA 90720
(213) 493-4440

**Children of Aging Parents**
**c/o Wagner Program**
15600 Mulholland Dr.
Los Angeles, CA 90077
(213) 476-9777 x 215

**Caregivers Support Group**
**Jewish Family Service**
330 North Fairfax
Los Angeles, CA 90036
(213) 937-5900

**Caregiver Support Group**
**OPICA**
11759 Missouri
Los Angeles, CA 90025
(213) 478-0226

**You & Your Aging Parents Support Group**
**Pico Robertson Storefront**
**Jewish Family Service**
8838 West Pico Blvd.
Los Angeles, CA 90035
(213) 271-3306

**Caregiver Support Group**
**El Camino Hospital Center on Aging**
777 Cuesta Drive, PO Box 7025
Mt. View, CA 94039-7025
(415) 966-9222

**Caregiver Support Group**
**Jewish Family Service**
12821 Victory Blvd.
N. Hollywood, CA 91606
(818) 984-1380

**Adult Children of Aging Parents**
**South Bay Family Therapy Center**
37053 Cherry St., #204
Newark, CA 94560
(415) 783-1080 (415) 794-4694

**Adult Children of Aging Parents**
200 Newport Center Drive, #204
Newport Beach, CA 92660
(714) 759-9363

**Caring for Aging Relatives**
**c/o Wilkinson Multipurpose Sr. Cr.**
8956 Van Alden
Northridge, CA 91324
(818) 701-0144

**Families of Elders Support Group**
**Help of Ojai, Inc.**
PO Box 621
Ojai, CA 93023
(805) 646-9752

**Adult Children of Aging Parents**
**St. Joseph Hospital Community Outreach**
1100 West Stewart Drive
Orange, CA 92668
(714) 771-8243

**Support Group for Children of Seniors**
**Palo Alto Senior Center**
450 Bryant St.
Palo Alto, CA 94301
(415) 327-2811

**Caring Children of Aging Parents/The Canterbury**
5801 Crestridge Road
Palos Verdes, CA 90274
(213) 378-8281

**Children of Aging Parents**
**St. Jude Hospital**
1012 Marina Drive
Placentia, CA 92670
(714) 996-2381

**180**

**Adult Children of Aging Parents**
PO Box 17366
San Diego, CA 92117
(619) 483-5100

**Family Survival Project**
425 Bush Street, Suite 500
San Francisco, CA 94108
(800) 445-8106 (415) 434-3388

**Children of Aging Parents (CAPS)**
**Goleta Valley Hospital, Ashton Center**
5333 Hollister Ave.
Santa Barbara, CA 93111
(805) 965-1001

**Caring Children of Aging Parents**
25550 Hawthorne Blvd., #212
Torrance, CA 90505
(213) 375-1968

**Coalition of Adults with Elderly Parents**
**Ventura Senior Outreach Services**
420 East Santa Clara St.
Ventura, CA 93001
(805) 652-7820

**AGE**
4525 West Tulare Ave.
Visalia, CA 93277
(209) 732-9826

**National Association of Caregivers of America**
3060 East Bridge, #342
Brighton, CO 80601
(303) 659-4463

**Caregiver Support Group**
**Colorado Generations, Inc.**
180 Cook St., Suite 117-E
Denver, CO 80206
(303) 231 -6370

**Adult Children with Aging Parents**
**Greeley Medical Clinic, Gerontology**
1900 Sixteenth St.
Greeley, CO 80631
(303) 350-2406

**South Metro Denver Caregivers Support Group**
Institute for Creative Aging
6325 South University Blvd.
Littleton, CO 80121
(303) 794-2683

**181**

**Families Caring for Elderly
Relatives
Adult Day Care Center,
Newark Hall**
University of Delaware
Lovett & Academy Sts.
Newark, DE 19716
(302) 731-9058

**AARP Caregivers Network**
1909 K Street, NW
Washington, DC 20049
(202) 728-4675

**Answers on Aging
Upper Level**
3363 18th Street, NW
Washington, DC 20010
(202) 234-7781

**HUD Elder Care Support
Dept. Housing & Urban
Development**
451 Seventh St.. SW, Room 5128
Washington, DC 20410
(202) 755-0523

**Adult Children of Aging
Parents
Jewish Community Center**
1401 West Royal Palm Road
Boca Raton, FL 33486
(407) 395-5965

**Clearwater Adult Day Care
Center
Neighborly Senior Services**
210 Ewing Ave.
Clearwater, FL 34616
(813) 443-1560

**NE Alzheimer's Day Care
Center**
227 NW Second Street
Deerfield Beach, FL 33441
(305) 480-4462

**For Those Who Care
Caregiver Education Program
Lee Memorial Hospital**
2776 Cleveland Ave.
Fort Myers, FL 33902
(813) 336-6786

**Caregivers Support Group
Older Americans Council**
1024 NE 14th St.
Gainesville, FL 32601
(904) 377-2790

**Adult Children of Aging
Parents**
100 Pasadena Avenue, North
St. Petersburg, FL 33710
(813) 345-0148

**182**

The Family Connection
Hawaii County Office of Aging
34 Rainbow Drive
Hilo, HI 96720
(808) 961-3747

Honolulu Gerontology
Program
Child & Family Service
550 South Beretania St.
Honolulu, HI 96813
(808) 537-2211

Handle With Care Caregivers
Support Group
Lutheran Community Services
800 West Oakton
Arlington Heights, IL 60600
(312) 253-3710 x 253

When Parents Grow Old
United Charities of Chicago
14 E. Jackson
Chicago, IL 60604
(312) 435-4175

Children of Aging Parents
Vermilion Mental Health
Center
605 North Logan
Danville, IL 61832
(217) 442-3200

Children of Aging Parents
Riverside Medical Center
350 North Wall St.
Kankakee, IL 60901
(815) 933-1671

Children of Aging Parents
508 Park Avenue, East
Princeton, IL 61356
(815) 872-2261

Caregiver Support Groups
Skokie Office on Aging
5140 Galitz Street
Skokie, IL 60077
(312) 673-0500

Caregiver's Support Group
Council on Aging
PO Box 97
Dillsboro, IN 47018
(812) 432-5215

Children of Aging Parents
Park Center, Admin. Building
909 East State Blvd., Rm. B 123
Fort Wayne, IN 46805
(219) 482-9111

**Support Group for Families
of Aging Relatives
Jewish Community Center**
6701 Hoover Road
Indianapolis, IN 46260
(317) 251-9467

**Alzheimer's Support Group
Tippicanoe Council on Aging**
533 Main St.
Lafayette, IN 47901
(317) 742-5109

**Children of the Elderly
Alpha Center**
315 South Monroe
Muncie, IN 47305
(317) 286-2800

**Caregiver Support Groups
Area Agency on Aging**
808 River
Decorah, IA 52101
(319) 382-2941

**Family Support Group & Easy
Aging
Fountain West Health Center**
1501 Office Park Road
West Des Moines, IA 50265
(515) 223-1223

**Families or Caregivers Under
Stress
Prairie View, Inc.**
1901 E. First St.
Newton, KS 67114
(316) 283-2400

**Family Support Group
Johnson County Area Agency
on Aging**
301 A. S. Clairborne
Olathe, KS 66062
(913) 782-7188

**Care & Responsibility for
Elderly Relatives-CARER**
644 North Bluff, #1
Wichita, KS 67208
(316) 686-1205

**Elder Care Solutions**
1220 Bardstown Road
Louisville, KY 40204
(800) 633-5723 (502) 452-9644

**Adult Children Caring for
Elderly Parents Together
(ACCEPT)
Greenbrier Hospital**
201 Greenbrier Blvd.
Covington, LA 70433
(504) 893-2970

**184**

Caregiver Support Group
Western Area Agency on
Aging
PO Box 659, 465 Main St.
Lewiston, ME 04240
(207) 482-0976

Key East Adult Day Caregiver
Support Group
Department of Aging
7401 Holabird Ave.
Baltimore, MD 21222
(301) 887-7245

Caregivers for the Elderly
Support Group
Office on Aging
145 North Hickory Ave.
Bel Air, MD 21014
(301) 838-2552

Caregiver Support Group -
Senior Center
Baltimore County Dept. of
Social Services
501 North Rolling Road
Catonsville, MD 21228
(301) 887-2516

Elder Love Support Group for
Caregivers
Washington County Library
100 S. Potomac St
Hagerstown, MD 21740
(301 ) 797-7373 (301) 790-0883

People Who Care
Office on Aging & Health
Dept.
450 West Dares Beach Road
Prince Frederick, MD 20678
(301) 535-4606

You and Your Aging Parent
North Shore Elder Services
484 Lowell Street
Peabody, MA 01930
(617) 535-6220

CFS Adult Day Care
Family Support Group
2455 Wastenaw Ave.
Ann Arbor, MI 48104
(313) 996-0407

Coping With Aging Parents
Holy Cross Hospital, c/o Social
Work Dept.
4777 E. Outer Drive
Detroit, MI 48234
(313) 369-9100

**Children of Aging Parents
Valley Court Comm. Cr.**
201 Hillside Court
East Lansing, MI 48823
(517) 337-6489

**Caregivers Support Group
Center for Gerontology**
303 W. Water St., Suite 100
Flint, MI 48503
(313) 767-7080

**Children with Aging Parents**
c/o 2418 Tanbark Ave.
Flint, MI 48532
(313) 732-3594

**As Parents Grow Older**
c/o 821 Seventh St.
Port Huron, MI 48060
(313) 984-5061

**Hand in Hand
Adult Children of Aging
Parents**
19785 W. Twelve Mile Rd.,
Ste. 102
Southfield, MI 48076
(313) 599-1691

**Caring for Aged Loved Ones
Herrick Memorial Health
Center**
500 E. Pottawatamie St.
Tecumseh, MI 49289
(517) 423-6000

**Phone Home Caregivers
Support Group
North Itasca Hospital**
Pine Tree Drive
Big Fork, MN 56628
(218) 743-3177

**Cambridge Caregivers
Support Group
7-E Area Agency on Aging**
224 South Ashland
Cambridge, MN 55008
(612) 689-4071

**Caregiver Support Group
Sioux Valley Hospital Adult
Day Care**
1324 Fifth St., N.
New Ulm, MN 56073
(507) 354-2111

**Senior Care Management**
256 S. Robertson Blvd, Suite 709
Beverly Hills, CA 90211
(213) 288-0059 (213) 288-0301
FAX

**Geriatric Counseling**
22318 San Joaquin Dr, W.
Box 5036
Canyon Lake, CA 92380
(714) 244-6680

**The Senior Connection**
510 S. Manzanita Ave.
Carmichael, CA 95608
(916) 972-1114

**PCI - Department of Health
Education**
5856 Corporate Ave.
Cypress, CA 90630-4729
(714) 229-2614

**Senior Care Network of
Huntington Memorial Hospital**
837 South Fair Oaks Ave.,
Suite 100
Pasadena, CA 91105
(818) 397-3110

**Family Gerontology
Association**
1427 Seventh Street, Suite 3
Santa Monica, CA 90401
(213) 458-9446

**Alzheimer Care Management
Associates**
19225 Rosita Street
Tarzana, CA 91356
(818) 342-3136 (818) 708-8538

**Gerontology Associates**
19225 Rosita Street
Tarzana, CA 91356
(818) 342-3136 (818) 708-8538

**Institute For Creative Aging**
PO Box 3725
Littleton, CO 80161
(303) 795-9682

**Geriatric Counseling
Associates**
441 Orange St
New Haven, CT 06511
(203) 785-1496

**187**

**Elder Family Service of
Connecticut**
191 Post Road West
Westport, CT 06880
(203) 221-2639 (203) 329-2750

**The Family Link**
PO Box 11791
Fort Lauderdale, FL 33339
(305) 566-7086

**Geriatric Home Care Coord.**
200 178th Drive #506
North Miami Beach, FL 33160
(305) 931-5833

**Eldercare of Pinellas, Inc.**
PO Box 4166
Seminole, FL 34642
(813) 397-0003

**T.L.C. for Seniors, Inc.**
13896 Dominica Dr.
Seminole, FL 34646
(813) 595-2000 (800) 729-8907

**Care Solutions, Inc. (CSI)**
Five Concourse Pkwy, Suite 810
Atlanta, GA 30328
(404) 393-7366

**Elder Link Inc**
2000 N. Racine, Suite 2182
Chicago, IL 60614
(312) 929-4514

**Aging/Options!**
171 Franklin Road
Glencoe, IL 60022
(708) 835-3183
FAX (708) 835-8413

**Geriatric Resource
Consultants, Inc.**
160 Cary Ave.
Highland Park, IL 60035
(708) 432-3490

**Senior Citizens Care
Management, Ltd.**
2000 W. Pioneer Parkway,
Suite 24
Peoria, IL 61615
(309) 693-5511

**Geriatric & Family Consultants**
3637 Rosewood Drive
Fort Wayne, IN 46804
(219) 432-2150

**Easy Aging**
921 39th St.
West Des Moines, IA 50265
(515) 223-0014

**188**

Elder Care Solutions/Home
Mgt. Service
1220 Bardstown Road
Louisville, KY 40204
(502) 452-9644 (800) 633-5723

Aging Network Services, Inc.
4400 East-West Highway,
Suite 907
Bethesda MD 20814
(301) 657-4329 (301) 951-8589

Emerging Lifestyles, Inc.
5659-C Harpers Farm Road
Columbia, MD 21044
(301) 997-1911

Creative Alliance
135 S. Huntington
Boston, MA 02130
(617) 731-1414

Caregiver Connection
1415 Granger
Ann Arbor, MI 48104
(313) 995-5022

Dakota Area Resources &
Transportation for Seniors
(DARTS)
60 E. Marie, Suite 210
West St. Paul, MN 55118
(612) 455-1560
FAX (612) 455-3901

ElderAssist
4218 Sarpy Avenue
St. Louis, MO 63110
(314) 533-7005

Parentcare
Clocktower Village
643 North 98th St., Suite 253
Omaha, NE 68114
(402) 390-9323 (800) 747-8818

Lend-A-Hand Program, Inc.
400 Utah St
Boulder City, NV 89005
(702) 294-2363

Sensible Options for Seniors
(SOS)
4-01 Summit Ave.
Fair Lawn, NJ 07410
(201) 796-6549

**All Things Relative**
Wallerstein Center
2401 White Plains Road
Bronx, NY 10467
(212) 653-0593

**Geriatric Care Consultants**
218 Rockaway Turnpike, Suite 217
Cedarhurst, NY 11598
(516) 374-4860

**Dolen Consulting Systems**
290 Quaker Road
Chappaqua, NY 10514
(914) 238-3261

**Comprehensive Care Management:**
**Advocacy for Aging**
15 Canterbury Road
Great Neck, NY 11721
(516) 829-7726 (212) 995-8762

**RISE-Referral, Info. & Support Services/Elderly**
Winthrop University Hospital
222 Station Plaza, Suite 330
Mineola, NY 11501
(516) 663-2920

**Directions in Aging**
1-B Quaker Ridge Road
New Rochelle, NY 10804
(914) 636-7347

**Comprehensive Care Management:**
**Advocacy for Aging**
201 East 17th St, Apt. 4A
New York, NY 10003
(212) 995-8762 (516) 829-7726

**The Connecting Hand**
286 Center Street
Oceanside, NY 11572
(516) 678-8665 (800) 525-8125

**Senior Care Connection**
2220 Burdett Ave
Troy, NY 12180
(518) 272-1777

**H.E.L.P. for Elders, Inc.**
812 Bromton Dr
Westbury, NY 11590
(516) 334-1131

**Senior Services, Inc**
836 Oak St, Suite 320
Winston-Salem, NC 27101
(919) 725-0907

**Third Age Life Center**
Baptist Medical Center
3300 NW Expressway
Oklahoma City, OK 73112
(405) 949-4140

**Eldercare Geriatric Services**
8329 High School Road
Elkins Park, PA 19117
(215) 635-6849

**Geriatric Planning Services**
Main Line Federal Bldg. #201
2 South Orange St.
Media, PA 19063
(215) 566-6686

**Senior Care Consultants**
5645 Marlborough Road
Pittsburgh, PA 15217
(412) 421-9171

**Sterling Care Counseling, Inc.**
962 Washington Road
Pittsburgh, PA 15228
(412) 344-5011

**Wise Generation Resources, Inc.**
100 Denniston Avenue
Pittsburgh, PA 15206
(412) 441-4342

**Eldercare Geriatric Services**
435 E. Lancaster Ave., Suite 211
St. Davids, PA 19087
(215) 688-5579

**Intervention Associates**
PO Box 572
Wayne, PA 19087
(215) 254-9001

**Care Options for the Elderly**
304 Seaton Lane
Falls Church, VA 22046
(703) 237-9048

**Michigan Self-Help
Clearinghouse**
109 W. Michigan, Suite 900
Lansing, Ml 48933
(517) 484-7373
(800) 752-5858 in Ml

**Americans For Generational
Equity (AGE)**
608 Massachusetts Ave. NE,
1st Fl.
Washington, DC 20002
(202) 686-4196

**191**

**Association Of Informed
Senior Citizens**
560 Herndon Pkwy, #110
Herndon, VA 22070

**Center For The Study Of
Aging (CSA)**
706 Madison Ave.
Albany, NY 12208
(518) 465-6927

**Center For Understanding
Aging (CUA)**
**Framingham State College**
Framingham, MA 01701
(508) 626-4979

# RELATED SERVICES

**Friendship House**
615 Three Eagles St.
Colorado Springs, CO 80906
(719) 473-9430
*Adult Day Care*

**Lifespan Adult Day Health
Center**
570 Main St
Pennsburg, PA 18073
(215) 679-7977
*Nursing Services, Personal Care
(Additional Services Available)*

**The Greatest of Ease Company**
2443 Fillmore St, Suite 345
San Francisco, CA 94115
(415) 441-6649 (800) 845-1208
*Rehabilitation Products to Help
People Live Independently.
Free catalog.*

**Fairlane Home Medical
Supply**
**Henry Ford Health System**
24445 Northwestern Hwy., #110
Southfield, MI 48075
(313) 277-6000
*Durable Medical Equipment &
Hospital/Home Care Supplies*
Helpline: (313) 972-1640
*Emergency Response System for
Older Adults Living Alone*

**The Family Link**
PO Box 11791
Ft. Lauderdale, FL 33339
(305) 566-7086
*Geriatric Consultants Care
Managers*

**192**

**Aging Network Services, Inc.**
4400 East-West Highway,
Suite 907
Bethesda, MD 20814
(301) 657-4329 (301) 951 -8589
*Consultation, Counseling, Care*
*Management. Referrals to Care*
*Managers anywhere in U.S.*

**Lend-A-Hand Program, Inc.**
400 Utah Street
Boulder City, NV 89005
(702) 294-2363
*Help Elderly Remain At Home*

**Health Care Services Systems**
PO Box 927
Philadelphia, PA 19105-0927
(215) 972-7009
*Health Education, Research &*
*Consultation for Health Care*
*Providers. Seminars Workshops*
*& Store-Front Health Education*
*Center*

**The Care Connection**
12420 Warwick Blvd, Bldg 6D
Newport News, VA 23606
(804) 599-8087
*Geriatric Care Consultants*

**Doolan-Glass Associates**
1700 Sansom St., Suite 701
Philadelphia, PA 19103
(215) 564-5868
*Counseling-Individual, Family,*
*Group—Home Visits Available*

**The Memory Institute, Inc.**
1015 Chestnut Street, Suite 1212
Philadelphia, PA 19107
(215) 923-8378
*Treatment for Individuals Early/*
*Middle Stages. Alzheimer's*
*Evaluation, Ongoing Medical*
*Monitoring, Newer Medications*

**Golden Crescent Area Agency**
**on Aging**
Victoria Regional Airport,
Building 102
PO Box 2028
Victoria, TX 77902
(512) 578-1587
*Emergency Response System -*
*Lifeline Program. Other Services*
*to the Elderly*

**Kelly Assisted Living**
999 West Big Beaver Road
Troy, MI 48084
(313) 362-4444
*Home Health Services*

**193**

**Dakota Area Resources & Transportation (DARTS)**
60 E. Marie, Suite 210
West St. Paul, MN 55118
(612) 455-1560
FAX (612) 455-3901
*Home Health Services, medical claims assistance and more.*

**V.I.P. Companion Care**
189 Haddonfield-Berlin Road, S-100
Gibbsboro, NJ 08080
(609) 346-4484
*Companion Care & Domestic Support*

**DBA Contemporary Home Care Services**
200 Old Country Road, Suite 200
Mineola, NY 11501
(516) 294-6565
*Home Health Care*

**HomeHealth Inc.**
410 Bath Road
Bristol, PA 19007
(215) 785-5244 (215) 345-4226
*Home Health Services*

**J.E.V.S. Home Health Care**
1330 Rhawn Street
Philadelphia, PA 19111
(215) 728-4411 (215) 728-4400
*Home Health Care - Personal Care, Meal Preparation, Companionship*

**Special Care, Inc.**
707 Bethlehem Pike
Philadelphia, PA I91 18
(215) 233-3962 (215) 233-5385
*Home Health Services & Home-makers*

**Independent Living, Inc.**
437 S. Yellowstone Dr., #208
Madison, WI 53719
(608) 274-7900
*Home Health, Home Chore, Meals, Friendly Visitors & More*

**Duraline Medical Products**
7-13 E. Main Street
PO Box 67
Leipsic, OH 45856
(419) 943-2044 (800) 654-3396
*Incontinent Products & Skin Care Products*

**194**

**Long Term Care Connection**
Green and Westview
Philadelphia, PA 19119
(215) 843-4855
*Ombudsman - Nursing &*
*Personal Care. Homes and*
*Consumer Advocacy*

**Pico Robertson Storefront**
Jewish Family Service
8838 West Pico Blvd.
Los Angeles, CA 90035
(213) 27 1 -3306
*Info. & Referral, Transportation,*
*Counseling for Caregivers*
*Care Management, etc.*

**Senior Care Network**
**Huntington Memorial Hospital**
837 South Fiar Oaks Ave,
Suite 100
Pasadena, CA 91105
(818) 397-3110
*Home Care Plus, Long Term*
*Care Insurance Program,*
*Consumer Education,*
*Coordinated Care*

**Professional Nursing**
**Home Placement Services**
19225 Rosita Street
Tarzana, CA 91356
(818) 342-3136 (818) 708-8538
*Nursing Home Placement,*
*Counseling, Assessment, etc.*

**Elder Care Solutions Home**
**Management Service**
1220 Bardstown Road
Louisville, KY 40204
(502) 452-9644 (800) 633-5723
*Home Health Services, Info. &*
*Referral. Nursing Home*
*Placement, Assessments,*
*Care Management*

**SAGE**
50 DeForest Ave.
Summit, NJ 07901
(201) 273-5550
*Info. & Referral, Adult Day Care*

**Family Support Services**
**Good Samaritan Hospital-**
**Medical Center**
1015 NW 22nd Ave, N-300
Portland, OR 97210-5198
(503) 299-7348
*Information & Referral for*
*Caregivers. Respite Care,*
*EducationTrainingforCaregivers*

**195**

**St. Jude Medical Center
Caring Children of Aging
Parents**
101 E. Valencia Mesa Dr.
Fullerton, CA 92635
(714) 871-3280 x 3323
*Caregiver Support Group, Other
Health Services*

**Catholic Charities**
1049 Market Street, 2nd Floor
San Francisco, CA 94103
(415) 864-7400
*Home Care, Adult Day Care*

**Help Unlimited, Inc.**
PO Box M
Watertown, CT 06795
(203) 274-7511
*Companion & Support Services
for Elderly and/or Convalescent*

**Norrell Health Care**
4239 War Memorial Dr.
Suite 304
Peoria, IL 61114
(309) 682-7291
*Home Health Services*

**Coping With Aging Parents
Adult Well-Being Services:**
2111 Woodward
401 Palms Bldg.
Detroit, MI 48221
(313) 961-5055
*Varied Services for Elderly &
Caregivers*

**Illinois Self-Help Center**
1600 Dodge Avenue
Suite S-122
Evanston, IL 60201
(800) 322-MASH (312) 328-0470
*Self-Help Clearinghouse
(National Info)*

**Well Spouse Foundation
Support Groups**
PO Box 28876
San Diego, CA 92128
*Chapters in many states and
areas*

**California Self-Help Center
U.C.L.A. Psychology Dept.**
405 Hilgard Avenue
Los Angeles, CA 90024
(213) 825-1799 (800) 222-LINK
*Self-Help Clearinghouse info for
California.*

**196**

The Sandwiched Generation
Association
Good Sheperd Lutheran
Church
22nd & Washington Blvd
Wilson Borough, PA
(215) 865-6565
*Groups in Bethlehem, Allentown,
Easton*

Lyndhurst Support Group
St. Clare's Church
Brainard & Mayfield Roads
Lyndhurst, OH 44124
(216) 881-1600 x 275
*Alzheimer groups*

Caregivers Under Stress
Clute Building of Arnot Ogden
Memorial Hospital
Ivy Street
Elmira, NY 14901
(607) 737- 1351
*Sharing & Education*

Caring for Caregivers
LIGHTHOUSE at Community
67 Highway 37 West
Toms River, NJ 08753
(908) 240-8200
*6 week sessions several times a
year*

Your Aging Parent & You
Chilton Memorial Hospital
97 West Parkway
Pompton Plains, NJ 07444
(201) 831-5160 (201) 831-5175
*Education & support series
offered twice a year*

Princeton Area Support
Group
Dorethea House
John Street and Paul Robeson
Place
Princeton, NJ
(609) 896-1494
*Alzheimer's group*

Support Group of Trenton
Lawrence Library
Route 1 and Darrah Lane
Lawrence Twp., NJ
(609) 396-1847
*Alzheimer's group*

Hamilton Area Support Group
Bethel Lutheran Church
150 Johnston Ave
Hamilton Twp., NJ
(609) 587-0834
*Alzheimer's group*

**197**

# MAGAZINES

*Aging Magazine*
Office of Human
Development Services,
Department of Health
and HumanServices,
200 Independence Ave. S.W.
Washington, DC 20201

*Modern Maturity*
Published by AARP
1909 "K" Street
Washington, DC 20049
800 523-5800

*Aging Today*
c/o American Society
On Aging
833 Market Street, Suite 512
San Francisco, CA 94103-1824

*Generations*
c/o American Society
On Aging
833 Market Street, Suite 512
San Francisco, CA 94103-1824

*Eldercare Business*
(A supplement to *Modern
Healthcare*)
740 N. Rush St.
Chicago, IL 60611

*Long-Term Care News*
1419 Lake Cook Road
Deerfield, IL 60015-5213

# INDEX

# About The Author

J. Michael Dolan was born on January 13, 1948, in Santa Monica, California. In 1977, after a lengthy career in the entertainment industry, he founded *Music Connection*, a music industry trade magazine published in Hollywood, California, and distributed nationwide. As an autodidact, he has relentlessly pursued the study of human development, psychology, and philosophy. Mr. Dolan has conducted numerous motivational seminars and has appeared on several radio and television talk shows. He is a frequent instructor for U.C.L.A.'s extension program and is often invited to speak at various colleges and functions.

You may correspond with the author directly by writing to:
J. Michael Dolan
P.O. Box 93879
Los Angeles, CA 90093

# NOTES

# NOTES